Leadership

*Building and Nurturing
a World-Class Team*

Steven Shuel D.C.

Copyright © 2021 by Steven Shuel D.C.

All rights reserved. This book or any portion thereof may not be reproduced or used in any manner whatsoever without the express written permission of the publisher except for the use of brief quotations in a book review.

Contents

Introduction 1

The Oak Haven Story 3

What Is Leadership? 7

Driving and Nurturing Workplace Culture 22

Extreme Ownership 45

General Leadership Principles 63

Build and Nurture a World-Class Team 95

Managing Conflict in the Workplace 139

Honest Conversations 180

How to Use This Material on Honest Conversation 231

Appendix 1 241

Appendix 2 245

Appendix 3 255

Acknowledgments 265

Introduction

Effective leadership is at the heart of every great organization.
Contrary to popular belief, great leaders are not born; they
are developed.
Thankfully, leadership is a learned skill.

IN THIS BOOK, WE WILL DISCUSS WHAT IT TAKES TO BE AN EFFECTIVE leader. But we will not just learn leadership principles; we will learn how to put them into practice for our own personal development, as well as for the betterment of Oak Haven Massage. We will challenge ourselves to:

- Set the bar high.
- Focus on high standards of excellence.
- Keep moving toward constant, never-ending improvement.

This book will also focus on what it takes to manage a team—to effectively develop and nurture others we've been asked to lead. So, what is a leader? What is expected of us if we're put in charge of a team?

Here's how professor and author Brené Brown defines a leader:

I define a leader as anyone who takes responsibility for finding the potential in people and processes, and who has the courage to develop that potential.

1

Leadership: Building and Nurturing a World-Class Team of Massage Therapists

We're not just developing ourselves. We're looking to develop the potential in each member of our team. We want to make them look good and use their full potential. By doing this, we're also making Oak Haven Massage better and better.

Putting these concepts on paper—writing this book—is a labor of love. I hope you, the reader, get something valuable from it—something that will make you a better person, a better leader, and a better member of the Oak Haven Massage team. Spend time with these ideas, and see what happens!

Steven Shuel

The Oak Haven Story

THE NEXT FEW PAGES, WRITTEN BY ALLISON MORENO, PRESIDENT OF Oak Haven Massage, tell the Oak Haven story. It's how it all began, but it's also how it evolved into a style unique to Oak Haven Massage and sought after by countless massage patients.

How a Failed Retirement Led to Oak Haven Massage

Dr. Steven Shuel likes to joke that he "failed at retirement."

In April of 2005, Dr. Shuel sold his chiropractic practice in Santa Paula, California, where he had practiced chiropractic since 1988. He and his wife, Kathleen, packed up all their belongings and moved to San Antonio, Texas, along with their four daughters. His retirement plan was to take a few years off and decide what he wanted to do with the next phase of his life. His two youngest daughters still had a few years of high school left, and the plan was to get the girls out of school, travel a bit with Kathleen, and enjoy life.

The plan was going pretty well—for five days. On the fifth day, he decided to get a massage. The massage was nice, but it was a little too "fluffy" for his taste. That massage triggered an idea.

What if he opened a massage center where clients could get a therapeutic level massage session similar to the sessions he and his staff did back in California? Most massage centers at this time were giving a more relaxing, spa-like massage. He thought there might be a market for a more medical style massage. He thought about this idea over the next several weeks and had several discussions with Kathleen. Then, in May 2005, he decided to open a new business, and Oak Haven Massage was born.

Oak Haven Massage opened its doors in November 2005, and Dr. Shuel officially ended his retirement. As of June 2018, they completed their 1 millionth massage session. They currently employ 210 employees, including 175 full-time massage therapists. So much for retirement.

What Is the Oak Haven Massage Method?

There are hundreds of different styles of massage and bodywork. Each style has its own story and its own reason for being developed. Bodyworkers learn the foundation of massage in massage school. Most massage schools teach a form of Swedish massage—the flowing, relaxing massage delivered in most spas.

As massage therapists branch out from their original foundation, they start to take more classes and engage in more training. Over time, they gradually begin to develop their own style of massage and bodywork. Massage is considered both an art and a science. Each therapist, like an artist, puts their own twist on whatever training they receive.

The Oak Haven Method of massage and bodywork was developed over the course of 33 years as Dr. Shuel received training himself and observed best practices of the therapists who were part of his clinic. The Oak Haven Method was developed by observing what specific maneuvers and procedures worked best with clients. The method developed as a gradual process over many years as bits and pieces of techniques were borrowed from many excellent therapists.

The Oak Haven Method can be seen as a patchwork of many different styles—styles that have been brought together into one integrated type of bodywork and then refined over 30+ years of treating clients. The method has, at its core, a flowing, deep pressure. The therapists use the height of the table, specific postures, and contact points to deliver deep pressure to the tissues. This method was developed as a pain reduction technique, but it also works well as a deep relaxation session.

The Oak Haven Method is a work in progress. It is an evolution that continues to change and adapt as we observe its impact on our clients. We are continually looking for different and better ways to improve and develop the method. We are always on the lookout for more effective ways to help our clients overcome the challenges of muscle-based pain patterns.

How the Oak Haven Method Was Born

The Oak Haven Method evolved through a happy accident. You might call it serendipity. In 1988, when Dr. Shuel took over a chiropractic practice in Santa Paula, California, along the Southern California coast, he noticed after about a year that his soft tissue techniques were very effective for his patients. Soft tissue techniques are the treatments aimed at the body's muscles, tendons, and ligaments. Most chiropractors at the time were focused mainly on the alignment of bones. Dr. Shuel noticed that by working on muscle tendons and ligaments, he could get much better results with many of his patients' pain patterns.

After two years of exploring these treatments, he hired his first massage therapist, Ramon, to assist him in his busy practice. Shortly after, he hired a second therapist, Debra. After his fourth year in practice, he knew he needed to hire a third massage therapist.

Here is where serendipity comes into the story. When he hired the third therapist, the clients rebelled. They did not like the style or methods this third therapist used. They told Dr. Shuel they only wanted Ramon or Debra to work on them. After several weeks of interviewing, Dr. Shuel was able to find another therapist who matched the style, strength, and methods of Ramon, Debra, and the Oak Haven style was born.

Of course, at the time, it wasn't called the Oak Haven Method; it was just "the style of massage the patients of Dr. Shuel like and are willing to pay for." But that was kind of a long, awkward name, don't you think?

Allison Moreno
Austin, Texas – August 2019

SECTION 1

What Is Leadership?

Only three things happen naturally in organizations: friction, confusion and underperformance. Everything else requires leadership.

—Peter Drucker

FOR PEOPLE AND ORGANIZATIONS, HIGH PERFORMANCE REQUIRES leadership. Apple, one of the most successful companies on the planet, understands that high performance and excellence do not occur naturally in business. The organization must be primed for high performance through leadership. When Apple established Apple University, its leadership training division, the company stated its mandate: *To defy the gravitational pull of organizational mediocrity.*

How do we defy mediocrity at Oak Haven Massage?

That is the purpose of leadership—to help yourself, the team, and the organization defy and resist mediocrity and underperformance.

Leadership has many roles. We will describe some of them in this book. But one clear role or purpose of leadership is to set a standard of excellence. Leaders set the bar, the standard of excellence, and then construct the team and internal processes to meet the challenge.

Leadership: Building and Nurturing a World-Class Team of Massage Therapists

One person who can teach us about leadership, about creating a winning team and defying the gravitational pull of organizational mediocrity, is a man named John Wooden.

Wooden was a three-time NCAA All-American basketball player in the 1930s. His Purdue University team won the NCAA championship in 1932. Wooden went on to become UCLA's men's basketball coach from 1948 through 1975. During one twelve-year period at UCLA, he won ten NCAA championships, including a record seven championship wins in a row. The coach with the next closest record won four NCAA championships. At one point, Wooden's team won a record 88 NCAA games in a row.

Wooden won the NCAA Coach of the Year award seven times. He was the first player to be named to the Basketball Hall of Fame as a player and a coach. During his long, successful coaching career, Wooden definitely defied and conquered the gravitational pull of mediocrity. His coaching style has been widely studied, and it is safe to say he focused on developing his team, creating champions with that unique management and coaching style.

Success Cycle

There is a lot we can learn from Coach Wooden's philosophy and methodology. One of his most famous and useful concepts is what he called the "success cycle." Success was something Wooden knew something about. As a player and a coach, he was wildly successful at the highest levels. Indeed, his record of success stands today. He saw that success didn't always have a long-lasting impact on those who achieved it. In fact, he would often refer to the "infection of success" and the "success cycle."

He observed that once success occurred, it didn't always lead to ongoing excellence. It often led to complacency and mediocrity.

What can we learn from John Wooden's concept of the success cycle?

Section 1: What Is Leadership?

For our purposes, let's look at what happens once success is obtained. One of Wooden's great insights was that success sometimes triggers a series of reactions that actually lead away from success. For some, success leads to complacency, arrogance, and mediocrity. When that occurs, success is short-lived—hence Wooden's saying, "Nothing fails like success."

Take a look at Appendix 1 in the back of this book. I have listed many of Coach Wooden's leadership and management concepts. But for now, I want to emphasize Wooden's concept that the infection of success leads to mediocrity.

If we are to wage a battle against *underperformance* (to use Drucker's word) and *organizational mediocrity* (to quote Apple's mandate), it is critical to have powerful, insightful, effective leadership that shows us the way.

By most definitions, Oak Haven Massage is considered a success. With 200 massage therapists working in five locations, 225 team members, and 650 massage sessions per day, we are undoubtedly one of the top massage centers in the country. Over the years, we have won numerous awards, including several Top Workplace, Best Place to Work, and Best Massage.

But here is a fair question: *What will success do to Oak Haven Massage?*

Will we be infected with our success? Will success take us toward complacency and mediocrity?

Or will we build on our success and have it take us toward continual improvement and excellence?

Wherever we are headed, it will be *leadership* that takes us there. My hope is that by focusing on the enduring principles of leadership, Oak Haven Massage will avoid the "gravitational pull of organizational mediocrity."

Together, we can:

- Set the bar high.
- Focus on standards of excellence.
- Keep moving toward constant, never-ending improvement.

All Leadership Begins with Self-Leadership

When we talk about implementing the principles of leadership at Oak Haven Massage, we need to assume that all leadership begins with self-leadership. We must first learn to lead and manage ourselves. It's essential to develop our own talents and capabilities before we attempt to manage others.

In his book *True North: Discover Your Authentic Leadership*, Bill George observed, "We have learned from working with many leaders that the hardest person you will ever lead is yourself."

Stephen Covey said, "Private victories precede public victories."[1]

Effective leadership must start with ourselves, with our own private victories. There is a hollowness to our leadership when we say one thing but do another. To lift up another, we must be standing on higher ground. We gain that higher ground as we seek our own development and expand our own skills and capabilities.

To quote Mahatma Gandhi, "Be the change that you wish to see in the world."

Coach John Wooden observed, "There is no more powerful leadership tool than your own personal example. In almost every way, the team ultimately becomes a reflection of their leader."

This matter of self-leadership is a critical topic. It is too large and too important to cover completely at this time. Instead, I will refer you to many worthwhile books and teachers on the topic. I have distilled much of what I have learned on the subject of personal development from a book called *Mindset Matters* by Lisa King. I highly recommend it to you.

Self-leadership is foundational. It provides the basis for team leadership and business leadership.

---

1 Stephen R. Covey, *The 7 Habits of Highly Effective People*, New York: Free Press, 2004, 43.

Section 1: What Is Leadership?

Three Broad Categories of Leadership

Let's look at these three broad categories of leadership:

- Personal leadership
- Team leadership
- Business leadership

Personal Leadership

Personal leadership is the process of expanding your own personal capabilities. Personal development is an ongoing process. Hopefully, we never finish the work of self-analysis and self-development. This process may start with your supervisors and managers at work giving you feedback regarding your performance. It may take the form of spending time with a personal mentor. It might involve seminars and workshops to help expand your current skill sets. You might focus on reading books that help you learn and develop.

Team Leadership

Once you have learned to look critically at yourself and expand your own capabilities, you are ready to work with teams in a leadership and management capacity. In this role, you will be responsible for managing other people's progress and development. You will train your team, follow up on their projects, and give them feedback. It's all part of the process of team leadership. This book focuses mainly on team leadership—how to develop and nurture the team you are asked to lead.

But at some point, you may move on from small teams to larger teams, and eventually to leading the business.

Business Leadership

Leading the business requires a different set of skills. When you lead a team, you are developing people, one individual at a time, all for the benefit and success of the team and thus Oak Haven. But when you lead an entire business entity, your focus is more on the vision and direction of the organization as a whole. Leading a business means you have to develop excellent communication skills in order to articulate that vision and direction to the entire organization.

Each of these leadership categories requires a slightly different aspect of leadership and a different set of skills.

Leadership or Management?

If you're leading a team, are you a *leader* or a *manager*? There are similarities and differences between the two.

First, how are they similar? Both are concerned with the development, training, and nurturing of people. Both include the development of business processes and the nurturing and driving of workplace culture. Both seek to bring out the best in others. According to Brené Brown:

> I define a leader as anyone who takes responsibility for finding the potential in people and processes, and who has the courage to develop that potential.

Second, how are they different? I often use the terms *leadership* and *management* interchangeably throughout this book. But let's look at some of the subtle differences between the two.

Leadership requires a vision of:

- What the division or company can be.
- Where we can go as a company.
- How we will get there.
- What will be required to arrive there.

A leader shares the vision of the company and where it is going. An effective leader shares the company's mission and *why it is going there*. Notice

Section 1: What Is Leadership?

that for both vision and mission, I use the word *share*. An effective leader must certainly already have the company's vision. A leader must also know and believe absolutely in the company's mission. But leaders also must be able to share or communicate the company's vision and mission. It's the sharing—the communication—that has the real power.

It's reasonable to ask, What good is it for a leader to have a powerful vision and a compelling sense of mission if it's not clearly and consistently shared and communicated?

Managers are the executors. They execute the company's vision. The ability to execute is a fundamentally different skill set than just knowing and seeing the vision—where the company needs to go. A manager is a visionary leader who is also excellent at executing, sharing, and teaching the vision. Managers know the company's vision and lead the business forward on the path that leads to that vision.

Managers train, nurture, and develop people. They look at the vision and the business processes that will fulfill that vision and seek to optimize every aspect of the company's operations through the people on their team.

There is an ongoing debate about the similarities and differences between leadership and management. Some excellent thinkers refuse to separate them and say there is no difference between them. Seth Godin, one of my favorite writers on business topics, says it this way: "If people have to follow you, you are a manager. If people want to follow you, you are a leader."

Stephen Covey says it this way:

> "In the words of both Peter Drucker and Warren Bennis, "Management is doing things right; leadership is doing the right things." Management is efficiency in climbing the ladder of success; leadership determines whether the ladder is leaning against the right wall."[2]

---

2 Covey, 101.

Leadership: Building and Nurturing a World-Class Team of Massage Therapists

I think the two have very similar qualities. But here is the difference. **Vision** and **mission** are the leader's responsibility. **Execution** belongs to the manager.

If You Want to Be a Leader, Examine Your Motives

In his excellent book *The Motive*, Patrick Lencioni describes two primary motives for someone who wants to be a leader:

1. The desire to be of service, to help develop, nurture, and guide others
2. The desire to be a leader for personal glory, aggrandizement, and prestige. These leaders want others to look up to them; they want to be seen as important and influential. They see leadership as the opportunity to do what they want to do without anyone holding them accountable.

One person becomes a leader to help others. The other sees leadership as a reward for years of hard work. One motive will lead to an effective, impactful leader; the other will create a leader whose impact is negligible.

There are many problems associated with people who become leaders for the wrong reasons. One of the problems is that in order for leadership to be effective and impactful, a person must engage in uncomfortable and challenging activities. Suppose someone becomes a leader for the wrong reasons. They often neglect or abdicate essential aspects of their role as a leader. Below are just a few challenging aspects of a leader's job, for the list is long and varied:

- Engaging in difficult conversations with team members; willing to have difficult discussions about ways a team member might need to adapt in order to become a more contributing member.
- Taking time to find fully compatible team members during the hiring mode rather than settling and filling an open slot.
- Removing team members who are not a good fit.

Section 1: What Is Leadership?

Leadership is a difficult job. It can be an uncomfortable job. If you are not engaged in leadership for the right reasons, you might find yourself avoiding the difficult parts of the job. Examine your motives for leadership. If you want to be a leader so you can nurture and build a great team, and are willing to do the hard work, you will love your role as a leader.

And remember, leadership and management are very much learned skills. It is a mistake to think that leaders are born.

Warren Bennis, often known as the "father of leadership," once wrote this:

> The most dangerous leadership myth is that leaders are born – that there is a genetic factor to leadership. This myth asserts that people simply either have certain charismatic qualities or not. That's nonsense. In fact, the opposite is true. Leaders are made rather than born.

Leadership Is Not a Title

Another important concept about leadership is that it does not require a title. John Addison, CEO and keynote speaker, said, "Leadership at its heart is more about influence than it is about position."

Titles such as manager, assistant manager, or lead therapist do not equate to leadership. Individuals can provide leadership in any position at Oak Haven Massage. A leader is someone who nurtures and brings out the latent potential in others. The title "manager" is not required to impact individuals in a positive way. Anyone can take on a leadership role at Oak Haven. They can help develop the people around them, and they don't need a formal title. Some of the best examples of leadership at Oak Haven are of people with no formal title. They just wanted to help their teammates grow and develop. They took it upon themselves to provide nurturing and training, often without additional pay or even recognition.

Leadership: Building and Nurturing a World-Class Team of Massage Therapists

How to Lead without a Title

Remember, leadership has three general buckets for our purposes—personal leadership, team leadership, and business leadership. The best place to start the process of leadership is with personal leadership—with yourself.

What can you do to work toward the best possible version of yourself? It's a logical place to start. How can you lead and grow the potential in someone else when you have not attempted to do it for yourself? Growth and development are a process. As you go through that process, you learn. Those lessons are extremely valuable as you work to develop others around you. And what kinds of things should you work on?

Everything.

- Work on personal character traits, such as **honesty**. Ask yourself if there are any areas you could be more honest in your interactions with others.
- Work on your **interpersonal relationships**. Try to eliminate any hint of gossiping. Are you speaking about others as if they were standing right next to you? Don't say anything about another person that you wouldn't say if they were in the room with you. Then take it a step further and defend those who are not present in the room. People have an intuitive sense that if you are trash talking others when they are not present, you are likely doing it to them when they are not in the room. Trust in relationships is a very important quality to cultivate in both personal and team situations.
- Focus on **personal excellence**. Learn every aspect of your job. Be able to function at the highest level of your position. If it's the front desk, that may mean understanding every aspect of the software program or developing the skills necessary to handle any customer problem or issue. If you're a massage therapist, personal excellence may mean knowing all the protocols and

16

Section 1: What Is Leadership?

having the anatomy structures committed to memory. It might mean going over the communication material and mastering the ability to set up and monitor a treatment program.

Teaching is also a good prerequisite for leading. At Oak Haven Massage, we can always use some assistance in our teaching programs. One of the incredible side benefits of teaching is that you must understand the concepts and maneuvers fully before you can teach them to others. So teaching becomes one of the best and fastest ways to gain personal mastery.

So, if you have aspirations to be a leader, start with yourself. Start with your own personal character and work on mastering your job. As you gain proficiency and competency, seek to teach others, either formally in a classroom or less formally in a personal mentoring session with a coworker who is asking questions or looking for help.

Spend time leading and developing yourself, and it will form a solid foundation for you to step into leadership and help develop other team members when the opportunity arises.

Managers Require Leadership Skills

Even though you don't need a title to be a leader, it is essential to have specific skills. Whether you are a leader or a manager, you must seek to gain the skill set required for the job. It's kind of like becoming a parent. You don't need a particular set of skills to become a parent. The hospital just hands you a child and requires no certificate of competency. But you have to start being a parent immediately, whether you have parental skills or not. You may need them when the baby starts screaming in the middle of the night.

We can become a manager (and hence a leader) in much the same way. Without any specific training, you might suddenly become a manager and feel a bit overwhelmed. It's a natural feeling.

So how do you get the necessary skill set to be a leader? How do you get it *before* you are put in a management position? This book will walk

17

Leadership: Building and Nurturing a World-Class Team of Massage Therapists

you through many of the principles and skills necessary to be an effective manager—the leader of your group.

Leadership Skill Set

You can learn how to be a leader. You can learn how to be a manager. Developing a leadership skill set is possible. Remember what I said about leaders—they are made and not born. The path to leadership includes gaining skills, but it also involves getting rid of specific habits or traits that might get in the way of becoming an effective leader. We'll take a look at those traits later, but first let's find out how to start developing a leadership skill set. It starts with *how you think* and *what you do.*

How You Think

Effective leaders think differently than ineffective leaders. I refer to this skill as *business philosophy.* Whenever you do anything as a manager, there is always a business philosophy behind it. Let me give you an example.

Let's say you become convinced that building trust is foundational for a leader. That is your business philosophy. You believe trust is critical. And when internalized, this philosophy will drive your actions.

> A receptionist tells you a salesperson is on the phone. How do you respond?
>
> "Tell them I'm not in."

or

> "Tell them I'm not available right now."

One response will erode trust, and one response will maintain or build trust. Our philosophical positions drive our actions. I could give a thousand examples of this.

18

Section 1: What Is Leadership?

You have a personal business philosophy, but each business and workplace also has its own business philosophy, a way of looking at its business and at people. It's how we think, it's what we think, and it's what we believe about people and the purpose of our business.

Our philosophy impacts how we treat people. It influences what is important to us and what is not. It shapes our priorities. Businesses also have a philosophy that shapes how they treat people and set their priorities. Oak Haven's philosophy will be obvious in this book, so be sure to watch for it.

What You Do

Now let's see how your business philosophy affects what you do. You will need to know this if you are a manager and want to become one. What you believe will affect your actions, including the following management skills:

- Hiring
- Communicating
- Building a cohesive team
- Onboarding new team members

- Training
- Giving feedback
- Firing
- Organizational Skills
- Operations

Your business philosophy will determine how you approach and carry out each of these skills. It is required in order to become a successful manager.

Intent Is Not Enough

You may say, *Well, it is always my intention to be skilled in these areas.* But intent is not enough to impact people at a high level.

One of the early lessons I learned about leadership and developing leadership skills was that internal intent was not enough to be an effective leader. In other words, just because I *wanted* to have a positive impact on the business and my team members did not mean I *had* a positive impact.

Leadership: Building and Nurturing a World-Class Team of Massage Therapists

A positive impact is based on a specific philosophy and a developed set of skills that go beyond intent.

Just like parenting, many effective leadership skills are learned on the job. Sometimes the only way to discover what is effective is by learning what is *not* effective. In other words, we learn by making mistakes. When we see the negative impact of a course of action, it causes us to stop and think about the situation and how the outcome might have been better.

We are left asking ourselves, *What could I have done differently? Where did I go wrong? How would I act if I had another chance?* And the next time a similar situation presented itself, we have a better idea of how to proceed.

Just ask any child who got a better deal in the parenting arena—the first child or the fourth. Most parents admit that they changed their parenting style quite dramatically from the first child to the fourth. Mistakes are often made at the start of parenthood. We see what works and what does not, and we shift our style. The younger kids usually benefit from this phenomenon.

Mistakes are often made when we first venture into management and become a leader for the first time. In both parenting and business, we are given a responsibility and stewardship without any real training or certification. We are forced to figure things out through trial and error.

And remember intent? Just because I *want* to have a positive impact on my child does not mean I *will* have a positive impact on my child. Just because I *want* to have a positive impact on my team members does not mean I *will* have a positive impact on them. There is a skill set involved in both parenting and management that can only be developed over time.

Here's another analogy. Your ultimate goal in raising your kids is that they eventually don't need you anymore. And your ultimate goal in managing is to teach your team so well and so completely that they don't need you anymore.

Section 1: What Is Leadership?

You Will Make Mistakes

Management and leadership are a learn-as-you-go process. You *will* make mistakes. But here's how to view them and how to react:

1. You will make mistakes. Accept it as truth, and be ready for it.
2. Acknowledge your mistakes. Learn from them, and move on.
3. When you make mistakes, practice an excuse-free apology.

When you make mistakes that involve people, it's usually essential to acknowledge your error. As part of the acknowledgment, you should also apologize, if appropriate. But make sure the apology is excuse-free. Take full responsibility for your mistake with no excuses for your actions or behavior.

In the digital version of this book, you can click on the link below and hear Scott Miller with the Covey Leadership Group speak on this topic.

Scott Miller – **Excuse Free Apologies** – https://sound-cloud.com/user-166537898/excuse-free-apologies

For a free digital version of this book, e-mail stevenshuel@gmail.com.

SECTION 2

Driving and Nurturing Workplace Culture

ONE OF THE MOST CRITICAL AND VITAL PARTS OF LEADERSHIP AND management is driving and nurturing workplace culture. A healthy culture at Oak Haven Massage starts with its leaders and spreads throughout the organization.

What Is Workplace Culture?

Culture is a collective agreement about the following:

- How we do things around here.
- How we think around here.
- How we treat people around here.
- What's important to us as a group.
- What we stand for.
- What we are trying to accomplish.

Culture is a commonly held set of values and principles that show up in people's everyday behavior. It's been said that *culture is what people do when no one is watching.*

Section 2: Driving and Nurturing Workplace Culture

Every organization has a culture. If an organization does not purposefully create the culture it wants, a culture will be created by default. An effective and wise leader will not leave the development of culture to chance.

Why Is Culture Important?

Workplace culture is a critical piece of the fabric of any business. Culture forms the foundation on which people do their work. If we at Oak Haven seek to bring out the best in team members, it's important to have a workplace culture that supports and encourages the following:

- Team members feel valued by management (leadership) and the business in general.
- We have an environment that creates mutual respect among team members.
- We have a sense of purpose and mission and effectively communicate it to our team members.
- We create an environment where team members are free to be who they are naturally and authentically.
- We provide a culture of excellence where team members seek to be the best possible versions of themselves.
- We have a culture of service that seeks to serve the needs of the customers at the highest possible level.
- We support a culture of "team first," which means zero tolerance for customers who act abusively toward any team member, and we are willing to dismiss abusive clients.
- Teamwork means we are all working for a common goal and are willing to do any job or task required to allow the business, including management, to function.
- We cultivate a positive relationship among team members by minimizing gossip.
- We maintain a low tolerance for drama among team members.

Leadership: Building and Nurturing a World-Class Team of Massage Therapists

Team members do their best work when our foundation is a culture of nurturing and supporting team members. We excel when there is a culture of excellence. And when team members are doing their best work, we create a world-class environment for our customers.

The most powerful competitive advantage of any organization is a compelling culture.[3]

Culture is important because it creates a competitive advantage. A supportive culture allows happy, supported team members to do their best work. Culture allows a responsive and high level of customer service. Excellent customer service starts with happy, supported team members in an environment where they feel empowered. Top-level customer service is a distinct competitive advantage for any business.

Culture also helps recruit top-level team members who want to associate with high-level teams. Our reputation at Oak Haven Massage goes before us when applicants apply for a position and get an interview. Potential applicants have heard about us. They have talked with our customers. They have spoken with former team members. Applicants look at our Google reviews, Yelp reviews, and Glassdoor reviews for insights into the culture of our company.

Workplace culture is also a critical factor in the retention of team members. From the front desk to therapists, team retention is an essential factor for business success. The degree to which we retain team members reflects directly on our excellent workplace culture.

Almost every aspect of Oak Haven Massage—the business, our leaders, our management—impacts company culture. And driving and nurturing a robust culture is one of the main functions of our leaders and managers. Every decision and all communication between leadership and their teams should be in light of its impact on company culture and employee morale.

---

3 Dusty Harts, quoted in Dr. Randy Ross, and David Salyers, *Remarkable: Maximizing Results through Value Creation*, Baker books, 2016.

Section 2: Driving and Nurturing Workplace Culture

Leaders and managers are constantly sending signals to our teams about how they are valued and respected. Every communication, every memo, every sign we put in the break room, every text message, and every company e-mail send signals about respect. Team members are quick to pick up on these cues. So take extra care when communicating with team members. Use a tone that accurately reflects care, concern, respect, and regard. These communications play a big part in Oak Haven's workplace culture. And team members tend to treat clients like they are being treated.

Each company has its own cultural DNA, so to speak. One culture may not work at another company. Practices and attitudes that allow you to flourish in one company or environment might be disastrous in another setting. The leadership and management methods of Oak Haven are highly culturally specific. The attitudes, philosophies, and methods practiced at Oak Haven and encouraged on these pages are specific to our company. They may or may not transfer to other businesses with different workplace cultures.

Let me give you a couple examples of what I mean.

We Value Team Members Over Toxic Customers

In some business environments, the customer is always right. If a team member does something to lose a customer, his or her job could be at risk. In our Oak Haven culture, we prioritize team members over toxic clients. We do not tolerate clients who use harsh, coarse, or insulting language with team members. We also refuse to accept any kind of rude or disrespectful attitudes toward our staff. Our philosophy is that life is too short to deal with people who act that way, who insult or verbally abuse our staff when they are disappointed. We may dismiss a client who acts that way.

We Accept Responsibility for Our Mistakes

Oak Haven Massage puts a very high priority on owning our mistakes and moving on. If someone admits to an error, even a potentially serious mistake, we have been known to counsel that person and help them keep their

25

position in the company. Of course, there are limits to our ability to over-look and move on, but we make every attempt when we can.

In other cultures and other business settings, admitting a mistake could get you fired.

An essential part of our culture is how we as an organization process mistakes. Do we punish mistakes? Do we look for someone to blame? Or do we seek to learn from a wrong decision? Do we process and move on, or do we dwell on the mistake and torment the person who made it?

It is always okay to talk about a bad decision. We dissect it, and then we learn from it. What could have been done differently? It is critical for the staff member to own his or her decision and the consequence of that deci-sion. Let's create a culture of *no blame*.

Own it, learn from it, and move on.

We Compensate Our Clients

At Oak Haven, we try our very best to give world-class service to our cli-ents. We have a very high standard we attempt to maintain. Unfortunately, on occasion, we fail to meet those standards. Sometimes we have an unhappy customer. When that happens, our customer service team is authorized to do anything and everything to make it right for that cus-tomer, including not charging the client for the underwhelming service he or she just received.

That is how we operate, but that same level of commitment to keep a customer happy could get a customer service person in trouble in other businesses.

The Oak Haven Way

We have an internal document here at Oak Haven Massage that is an important part of creating our culture. We call it the **Oak Haven Way card**. It's a small card the size of a business card that communicates concisely who we are and what we, as a group, believe. Our hope is that every team

Section 2: Driving and Nurturing Workplace Culture

member becomes familiar with it and carries it with them. I've included the card's contents here so you can get a feel for the tone of the message.

The Oak Haven Way

Why We Exist

Oak Haven Massage exists to enhance the lives of clients, team members, and shareholders and to make the world a better place **through the healing power of bodywork**.

Our Business Summary

Many people have a difficult time finding highly qualified massage therapists who are effective and don't waste your time or your money.

We take the guesswork out of finding highly skilled massage therapists by being super selective in our hiring process—we hire 1 out of 30 therapists we interview. Then we provide hundreds of hours of additional training for therapists each year. We want clients to have a world-class session every time.

Company Values

ELITE

E Exceed Customer Expectations

L Learn & Grow

I Integrity & Honesty

T Team Members Above Everything Else

E Enjoy and Have Fun

Leadership: Building and Nurturing a World-Class Team of Massage Therapists

Overall Philosophies

- We believe work should be more than a way to make money. We believe work is a vehicle for self-expression, personal growth, personal fulfillment, and service to humanity.
- We work to live, not live to work. Our work, while being personally fulfilling and a vehicle for service, should ultimately service ourselves and our family first.
- We believe work should be fun. Because we spend so much time at work, let's enjoy it.
- We hope the greatest reward for your involvement with Oak Haven is not what you get from it (salary, etc.) but what you become from it.

How to use **Oak Haven Way** cards:

1. Start every meeting with a review of some aspect of the material on the card.
2. Have team members integrate this thinking into their psyche and into the Oak Haven culture.
3. By continually reviewing the material, we send the message that this is not just stuff we write on a card and forget about. It's a way of life for us.

Below are some of the things we are doing internally to teach and reinforce the material on the card.

Teaching the Oak Haven Way:

1. Constantly attempt to reinforce the ideas in the Oak Haven Way card.
2. Make this material part of who we are as a company.
3. Don't ask team members to memorize or recite the material on the card.

28

Section 2: Driving and Nurturing Workplace Culture

4. Don't stop team members in the hallway and quiz them.
5. Start each meeting with a quote from the card on one aspect of the Oak Haven Way.
6. Look for ways to teach fundamentals at the start of every meeting or huddle.
7. Look to slowly, over time, embed these ideals.
8. Try to make the card reviews fun, inviting, and creative.
9. Aim to make the repetition of these fundamentals a habit.
10. Never stop teaching the fundamentals.
11. Make it your goal to see the Oak Haven Way become internalized among team members.

Theodore Roosevelt said: "Far and away the best prize that life has to offer is the chance to work hard at work that is worth doing."

We believe massage and bodywork is work that is indeed "worth doing." We believe in constant and never-ending improvement. We seek to continually establish a new set of standards in the massage and bodywork industry and then push to raise the bar.

Oak Haven Massage Fundamentals

1. **Be a lifelong learner.** Seek to learn and develop as a person, as a professional, and as a team member—a growth mindset matters.
2. **Exceed customers' expectations.** Go the extra mile, do what is best for the customer, handle problems fast, own every problem, and build rapport with the client. Seek to rise to the level of legendary service.
3. **When problems arise, resist placing blame.** Look for a system-wide solution that would prevent the problem. Talk about issues with those who have the authority to fix the problem.
4. **Accept responsibility for mistakes and lapses in judgment.** Everyone makes them. When errors are made, accept

29

Leadership: Building and Nurturing a World-Class Team of Massage Therapists

responsibility, learn from the mistake, and commit to a new and positive future.

5. **Assume positive intent.** Operate under the assumption that people are good, fair, and honest, and that the purpose behind their actions is positive. Set aside your own judgments and preconceived notions. Give people the benefit of the doubt.

6. **Help build up, support, and inspire fellow team members.** Refrain from gossiping. Inspire and make a difference in our co-workers' lives by helping them reach their full potential.

7. **Keep the commitments you make.** We believe business is ultimately about making and keeping promises. Earn the trust of co-workers and clients by keeping every commitment you make, no matter how small.

8. **Keep confidential information confidential.** It is critical to keep both client and team member information confidential.

9. **Deliver a world-class session every time.** Start every session on time, review client preferences before each session, and give the client his or her full time. Take good notes. Refrain from excessive talking. Give the client the session they want, not the session you would like.

10. **Look for points of customer friction you can eliminate.** Strive to make it easier for customers to do business with us.

11. **Work as a team.** Make decisions based on what is best for the customer. Refer to other therapists when appropriate. Remember, "a rising tide lifts all boats."

Let's look next at Oak Haven Massage's mission. It is an important part of our culture.

Section 2: Driving and Nurturing Workplace Culture

Mission Why We Talk About It

Oak Haven's mission is our "why." Why are we in business? Why do we get up in the morning? Why do we serve who we serve? We want to answer these questions so we can better serve our clients.

Here are some reasons we want to talk about the mission of Oak Haven Massage:

- Team members need to understand why we are in business.
- Team members need to know what business we are really in and who specifically we are serving.
- Team members need to know what makes Oak Haven unique and how we are different than other massage centers.
- Team members need to know that Oak Haven exists to serve our customers, but it also exists to serve the team.

A Mission That Matters

Do You Have a Job, a Career, or a Mission?

Have you ever pondered your relationship to the world of massage? When you think about your massage profession, do you consider it a job, a career, or a mission?

Let me explain what I mean.

A **job** is merely something we endure to get a salary.

A **career** is work that gives us prestige or position in society.

A **mission** (a purpose, a crusade) is work that is integral to our identity and meaning in life. It is an expression of who we are. Our mission has the potential to give us a sense of fulfillment, purpose, and meaning.

It's an interesting question to consider. *What is the world of massage for you—a job, a career, or a mission?*

- Do you want to make a difference in the world?
- Do you want to live a life of purpose and meaning?

Leadership: Building and Nurturing a World-Class Team of Massage Therapists

- Do you want to spend your days with work that matters?
- When you come home at night, do you want to feel that your work that day made a difference in people's lives?
- When your time on earth is finished, do you want people to say at your funeral, "This is a person who mattered, who made a difference"?
- Do you want people to miss you when you're gone?

If you answered yes to the above, that's good. Let's take a minute and explore what "making a difference" looks like.

The Man Who Changed His Life after Reading His Obituary

By Dov Greenberg

The world's most famous set of awards are the Nobel Prizes. Presented for outstanding achievement in literature, peace, economics, medicine and the sciences, they were created a century ago by Alfred B. Nobel (1833-1896), a man who amassed his fortune by producing explosives. Among other things, Nobel invented dynamite.

What motivated this Swedish munitions manufacturer to dedicate his fortune to honoring and rewarding those who benefited humanity?

The creation of the Nobel Prizes came about through a chance event. When Nobel's brother died, a newspaper ran a long obituary of Alfred Nobel, believing that it was he who had passed away. Thus, Nobel had an opportunity granted few people: to read his obituary while alive. What he read horrified him: the newspaper described him as a man who had made it possible to kill more people more quickly than anyone else who had ever lived.

At that moment, Nobel realized two things: that this was how he was going to be remembered, and that this was not how he wanted to be remembered. Shortly thereafter, he established the awards. Today, because of his doing so, everyone is familiar with

Section 2: Driving and Nurturing Workplace Culture

the Nobel Prize, while relatively few people know how Nobel made his fortune…

Thinking about how one's obituary is going to read can motivate one to rethink how he is currently spending his life. No eulogy ever says he/she dressed well, lived extravagantly, took fabulous vacations, drove an expensive car, or built the most expensive home. I never heard anyone praised for being too busy at work to find time for their children…

The people who are most mourned are not the richest or the most famous, or the most successful. They are people who enhanced the lives of others. They were kind. They were loving. They had a sense of their responsibilities. They were loyal friends and committed members of communities. They were people you could count on.[4]

Not all of us can be an Alfred B. Nobel. We all can't be Thomas Edison, who brought electricity to the masses. Not all of us can be Henry Ford, who changed the world through a new manufacturing process. Not all of us can be Elon Musk, who started an electric automobile company and a rocket manufacturing company. We can't all be Steve Jobs or Mark Zuckerberg. Not all of us can start an Amazon like Jeff Bezos. We may not be able to match these people's accomplishments, but we can still make a difference. We can still matter.

The Starfish Story: One Step towards Changing the World

By Peter Straube

Once upon a time, there was an old man who used to go to the ocean to do his writing. He had a habit of walking on the beach

---

4 Dov Greenberg, "The Man Who Changed His Life after Reading His Obituary,"
Chabad.org, https://www.chabad.org/library/article_cdo/aid/271383/jewish/
The-Man-who-Changed-his-Life.htm.

Leadership: Building and Nurturing a World-Class Team of Massage Therapists

every morning before he began his work. Early one morning, he was walking along the shore after a big storm had passed and found the vast beach littered with starfish as far as the eye could see, stretching in both directions.

Off in the distance, the old man noticed a small boy approaching. As the boy walked, he paused every so often and as he grew closer, the man could see that he was occasionally bending down to pick up an object and throw it into the sea. The boy came closer still and the man called out, "Good morning! May I ask what it is that you are doing?"

The young boy paused, looked up, and replied "Throwing starfish into the ocean. The tide has washed them up onto the beach and they can't return to the sea by themselves," the youth replied. "When the sun gets high, they will die, unless I throw them back into the water."

The old man replied, "But there must be tens of thousands of starfish on this beach. I'm afraid you won't really be able to make much of a difference."

The boy bent down, picked up yet another starfish, and threw it as far as he could into the ocean. Then he turned, smiled, and said, "It made a difference to that one!"[5]

We all have the opportunity to help create positive change, but if you're like me, you sometimes find yourself thinking, *I'm already really busy, and how much of a difference can I really make?* This is especially true when we're talking about addressing massive social problems such as world hunger or finding a cure for cancer, but it pops up all the time in our everyday lives

---

5 Peter Straube, "The Starfish Story: One Step towards Changing the World," *Events For Change*, https://eventsforchange.wordpress.com/2011/06/05/the-starfish-story-one-step-towards-changing-the-world/, adapted from Loren Eiseley, *The Star Thrower* (New York: Harvest Book Company, 1978).

Section 2: Driving and Nurturing Workplace Culture

as well. So when I catch myself thinking that way, it helps to remember the starfish story. You might not be able to change the entire world, but just like the boy and the starfish, at least you can change a small part of it for someone.

One of the most common reasons we procrastinate is because we see the challenge before us as overwhelming. An excellent way to counter that is to break down the big challenge into smaller pieces and then deal with those one at a time—one starfish at a time. To that one starfish, it can make a world of difference.

> A single, ordinary person still can make a difference – and single, ordinary people are doing precisely that every day.
> —Chris Bohjalian

What if we set the expectations for our impact on humanity in very reasonable and reachable terms? What if we set a goal to impact not the 7.7 billion people of the world, but those few we actually come in contact with every day? Would that be a reasonable, reachable goal?

Why don't we start by impacting the people who walk into Oak Haven Massage every day? Those are the people we can impact. We can make a difference in their lives.

Oak Haven Massage—Our Unique Niche in the Healthcare World

Let's talk about what we do at Oak Haven Massage.

The first and most obvious task we do is **give massage sessions**. I think we do an excellent job of delivering high-level Swedish and deep tissue massages. That will always be part of Oak Haven Massage.

However, quite a few massage establishments also offer good Swedish and deep tissue massages. Here's what makes Oak Haven stand out from the usual, standard massage center: our interest in *treating myofascial muscle-based pain patterns*. Looking for and treating the cause of muscle-based pain is what separates Oak Haven from the crowd. Let's expand on this idea.

Leadership: Building and Nurturing a World-Class Team of Massage Therapists

Effective treatment of a disease, condition, or pain pattern requires that we first understand **the cause of the pain or the dysfunction**.

Trying to treat a disease or pain pattern while not understanding the cause will waste a client's time and money. A failed treatment will also prolong them from getting proper treatment.

Example 1

Suppose someone had a diseased tooth and a horrible toothache. What would happen if we treated them with a beautiful pair of prescription eyeglasses? Of course, the treatment would not work. The toothache will only be resolved if the diseased tooth is addressed.

Example 2

What is the treatment for headaches? It depends on the cause of the headaches. If it is a brain tumor that's causing them, then the tumor must be removed. If an eye problem that requires corrective lenses is causing the headaches, then glasses are the proper treatment. If the headaches are a result of sulfites in wine, then the headaches can be resolved by eliminating sulfites from the diet. If headaches are a result of hormonal imbalance, hormones must be restored to normal levels. Likewise, if the headaches are from a myofascial source—muscles, tendons, or ligaments creating a trigger point area—the trigger point must be eliminated to resolve the headaches. The doctor can give pain medication to lessen the pain, but until the cause of the pain is addressed, the problem will likely persist.

Pain Patterns

Any pain pattern—headaches, shoulder pain, neck pain, back pain—can and does have many potential causes.

Our experience shows that half of all back, neck, shoulder, leg, knee, and foot pain are primarily muscle, tendon, and ligament problems.

36

Section 2: Driving and Nurturing Workplace Culture

A muscle-based problem requires a muscle-based solution, just as a dental problem requires a dental solution, or an eye problem requires an optical solution.

Clients deserve to have real solutions that address the cause of their muscle-based pain patterns.

Attempting to solve muscle-based problems by standard medical methods such as pain medication is ineffective because it does nothing to address the problem's source. Pain pills will not solve the problem any more than glasses will fix a toothache.

The question is this: Who will deliver these myofascial, muscle-based treatments? Certainly not...

- Medical doctors
- Nurses
- Physical therapists
- Acupuncturists
- Often not chiropractors
- Sometimes not even massage therapists

If these health professionals are not addressing the myofascial issues, *who will?*

Seth Godin asks a question that speaks to this issue facing massage therapists:

What If You Stopped?

What would happen to your audience if you shut the doors tomorrow? (I know what would happen to *you*, that's not my question... what would happen to them?)

What would happen to your customers and to your prospects if you stopped doing your work?

If you stopped showing up...would they miss you if you were gone?

37

If the airline went away, we'd just find another airline. If the cookie cutter politician went away, we'd just vote for someone else. If the typical life insurance agent...[6]

Those are great questions. Would our customers miss us? And who would do the work if we were not there?

The Role of Massage Therapists in Treating Pain Patterns

Massage therapists, in general, have not embraced the therapeutic possibilities of myofascial work. As professionals, they have opted to give feel-good, luxurious, relaxing sessions instead of the more aggressive and uncomfortable therapeutic-level sessions.

Massage started out as a soothing, relaxing modality, not a therapeutic modality.

Today, it is largely seen by the general public as a soothing, pampering modality.

From the 1940s through the 1960s, starting with Ida Rolf, massage and soft tissue work entered the therapeutic realm. From the 1970s on, various massage and bodywork practitioners added to our knowledge of the effectiveness of soft tissue methods as a therapeutic tool.

But in general, massage professionals today have little knowledge of the therapeutic benefits of massage and bodywork.

Part of the dilemma massage therapists face is that *the general public is often not aware of the effectiveness of massage therapy for treating many conditions.* When clients call for an appointment, they are seeking a standard, feel-good massage. Many clients have become resigned to the pain patterns they suffer. They often have been told they will need to live with the pain or

---

6 Seth Godin, "What If You Stopped?" *Seth's Blog*, https://seths.blog/2015/04/what-if-you-stopped/

Section 2: Driving and Nurturing Workplace Culture

need medication to reduce the pain. They are convinced that nothing will solve their problem.

It would be similar to people suffering from vision problems and optometrists were only trained to fit them with non-prescription sunglasses. Or it would be like people suffering from toothaches, and the dentist would only clean their teeth because drilling and filling cavities would cause too much pain. How sad it would be if a whole category of healthcare practitioners stopped treating what they identified. Patients with those conditions would not have an option to address and correct the cause of their pain and suffering.

My 33 years and 1.7 million treatments have convinced me that half of all musculoskeletal problems are treated effectively only by a qualified myofascial practitioner. Massage therapy is the profession that is best equipped to deliver the treatments for these conditions. If they do not treat these myofascial conditions, who will?

In March 2020, the COVID-19 pandemic hit the United States. Oak Haven and many other personal service businesses were mandated by the State of Texas to close. This situation left our clients with no options for treatment. Lindsey, our regional manager in San Antonio, shared her thoughts about this interesting time.

> As COVID hit in March, I wasn't sure what to expect for our business. I spent much of my quarantine time thinking about whether clients would even want to get a massage if we reopened. Close contact *is* our business, and I often let negative thoughts of a long-term closure consume me.
>
> We anticipated a late summer opening, but in late May, when the governor allowed sessions deemed medically necessary, my vote was to jump on the opportunity. We did just that, and on my first day back, I had renewed hope for Oak Haven Massage. BJ and I were the only ones answering phones at that time, and clients were doing everything they could to get their hands on a prescription for massage therapy.

I can't count the number of times a client said, "I've been waiting for y'all to re-open!" or, "I've missed you!" The fear instilled in the community during quarantine did not sway our most loyal clients who see our services as *essential*.

May 19, 2020 is a day I will never forget. The previous day, the governor announced that massage facilities could open to the general public. We sent out an e-mail to our clients announcing the good news, and our phones rang off the hook for five straight hours. It was the most blissfully stressful five hours! One client asked why it took so long to get through, and I explained that we didn't anticipate such a big response. The client replied, "Shame on you for not knowing your worth. You are Oak Haven Massage!" At that moment, I realized our clients truly missed us, and I am more confident than ever in the future.

I repeat, if we don't do this work, who will?

Let's summarize massage therapists' role in treating pain patterns.

- Effective treatment for any condition or pain pattern is a function of the cause.
- If the cause is abnormal muscle activity (trigger points), a myofascial treatment is mandatory.
- Because most of the healthcare world has no knowledge of how to treat these conditions, clients have become resigned to their pain. They have lost hope in finding a real solution to their problems.
- If we don't treat the condition, who will?
- We must train the next generation of myofascial practitioners to address these issues.
- We must educate the public about the effectiveness of myofascial work for many common conditions.

Section 2: Driving and Nurturing Workplace Culture

This is the situation we currently have in the massage world. We have a very specific problem with massive amounts of pain, dysfunction, and suffering and literally no one to treat the condition. To complicate the issue, the general public does not know that massage therapy is the best profession to correct those issues.

We know dentists are the only group trained to fix a tooth condition. But the general population doesn't know who to go to for muscle-based problems that, by many estimates, account for half of all doctor visits.

Oak Haven Massage is committed to and focused on two areas as they relate to these challenges.

1. Education

Oak Haven Massage is committed to educating massage therapists as well as the public.

We have in-house training facilities in San Antonio and Austin, where we offer more than 300 hours of training each year. We are also in the process of setting up a state-licensed massage school where we will train the next generation of bodyworkers.

2. Treatment of Specific Conditions

Many of our classes focus on training therapists to treat conditions, including:

- Headaches
- Neck pain
- TMJ pain
- Back pain
- Shoulder pain
- Arm pain
- Rib pain
- Low back pain
- Hip pain
- Leg pain
- Knee pain
- Foot pain

Accomplishing this may require shattering barriers and knocking down roadblocks. When it comes to shattering barriers, we can take inspiration from a young Englishman named Roger Bannister.

Leadership: Building and Nurturing a World-Class Team of Massage Therapists

Breaking Psychological Barriers

One of the great human athletic accomplishments occurred on May 6, 1954 in Oxford, England. Roger Bannister, a medical student from Oxford University, ran the mile in 3 minutes 59.4 seconds, setting a world record. Even more important, he broke the four-minute mile barrier, something athletes had eyed since the 1880s.

For 75 years, this barrier (the sub-four-minute mile) refused to be broken. Scientists had long taught that the human body was incapable of running a mile faster than four minutes, and 75 years of trying to break that barrier had confirmed it would never be broken.

But Roger Bannister did it. It was a tremendous accomplishment, indeed, but the story of this feat does not end there. Bannister's achievement taught us some important lessons. Just 46 days later, an Australian runner also ran a sub-four-minute mile. Within a year, three more people had broken the four-minute barrier.

What happened? Had training and human performance suddenly taken a quantum leap? Were these people part of a genetic breed of super-runners?

No. Something much more fundamental than super-genetics was at play. It was all about **belief**. What changed that day in May 1954 was that a psychological barrier crumbled. A long-held belief was shattered that day in Oxford.

Mindsets changed. What was impossible the day before was now possible, and person after person stepped up and did the impossible because one person showed them the way.

> *What a lesson for all humanity!*
>
> *What a lesson in the power of belief!*
>
> *What a lesson in shattering self-imposed limitations!*

Section 2: Driving and Nurturing Workplace Culture

What About You?

- What psychological barriers has society set for you as a massage professional?
- What barriers have you set for yourself?
- How can you recognize those barriers and set your performance on "shatter mode"?
- Everyone has a different psychological barrier to break as they seek to develop themselves and grow in the world of massage and bodywork. What is your psychological barrier in the field of massage?
- What psychological barriers are imposed by society at large? By the massage profession?
- Some barriers are self-imposed and become our own four-minute barrier that we alone can identify and shatter. What four-minute barrier have you already broken?

Just like the runners in Bannister's day, we don't know the upper limits of massage therapists' capabilities.

We do not yet know how great of an impact a massage therapist can have on humanity.

We do not know the upper limits of what a massage therapist can earn hourly or annually.

All we know is that we can have more of an impact on our clients than we now have.

How much more? That is yet to be determined.

Expanding Our Potential

Oak Haven Massage—who are we at our core? Who are we as a company when our hands are not on bodies? What do we think about and ponder when we reflect on our work? What are our aspirations as a group?

We can summarize who we are in two words—**expanding potential**.

Leadership: Building and Nurturing a World-Class Team of Massage Therapists

As a company, we are all about constant and never-ending improvement. That is a fancy way to say we are always seeking to learn, grow, and develop as professionals and as people. In short, we are about expanding our potential as human beings.

How far can Oak Haven go? We are not sure.

Raising the Bar

At Oak Haven Massage, we are seeking to raise the bar in two areas:

Customer Service – the way we interact with our clients.

Bodywork – helping clients function at their highest level.

Our intent is to set the standard in the industry for both customer service and bodywork. We are seeking to expand our potential to serve our customers at the highest possible level.

How high can we raise the bar on customer service? We don't know.

Our massage sessions are an attempt on our part to expand the potential of our clients. If clients suffer from pain in any form—headaches, neck pain, back pain, muscle dysfunction—they are not able to function at their highest level. If we can reduce the myofascial involvement through our muscle-based work, we are, in effect, expanding our clients' potential as human beings. Any person who has had debilitating headaches or back pain knows this is true.

So, as we go through our days, let's reflect on who we are at our core. Who are we when our hands are not on bodies?

*We are people who seek to **expand potential**—in ourselves, in our work, and in our clients.*

SECTION 3

Extreme Ownership

THIS BOOK IS PRIMARILY ABOUT MANAGEMENT—THE NURTURING of people, processes, and culture. A manager's unique focus is executing—getting stuff done. But an effective manager is also a good leader. In this section, we'll look at leadership and how it relates to management.

Most of the ideas and concepts in this section are a synopsis of the ideas in *Extreme Ownership*, an amazing book by Jocko Willink and Leif Babin. I highly recommend it and encourage you to read it on your own. We can relate many of their ideas to managing and leading at Oak Haven Massage.

8 Core Concepts of Leadership[7]

Let's look first at the core concepts of leadership. I have distilled eight of them from the book *Extreme Ownership*.

1. Leaders must own everything in their world; there is no one else to blame.
2. There are no bad teams, just bad leaders.
3. Good leaders don't make excuses.

---

7 Jocko Willink and Leif Babin, *Extreme Ownership: How Navy Seals Lead and Win*, St. Martin's Press, 2015.

4. Every team leader will make mistakes, and when that happens, the leader must confront those mistakes.
5. To be an effective leader in an organization, you must believe in the organization's mission and purpose.
6. It's crucial to lead both up and down the chain of command.
7. As team leaders, we should train junior leaders and then allow them to do their job. The goal of a leader should be to work themselves out of a job.
8. Be close with the team but not too close.

Now let's take a closer look at each of these leadership concepts and how they might apply to our work at Oak Haven Massage.

Core Leadership Concept #1

Leaders must own everything in their world; there is no one else to blame.

(From *Extreme Ownership*)
On any team, in any organization, all responsibility for success and failure rests with the leader. *The leader must own everything in his or her world.* There is no one else to blame. The leader must acknowledge mistakes and admit failures, take ownership of them, and develop a plan to win.

The best leaders don't just take responsibility for their job. They take Extreme Ownership of everything that impacts their mission. This fundamental core concept enables SEAL leaders to lead high-performing teams in extraordinary circumstances and win. But Extreme Ownership isn't a principle whose application is limited to the battlefield. This concept is the number one characteristic of any high-performance winning team, in any military unit, organization, sports team, or business team in any industry.

46

Section 3: Extreme Ownership

When subordinates aren't doing what they should, leaders that exercise Extreme Ownership cannot blame the subordinates. They must first look in the mirror at themselves. The leader bears full responsibility for explaining the strategic mission, developing the tactics, and securing the training and resources to enable the team to properly and successfully execute.

If an individual on the team is not performing at the level required for the team to succeed, the leader must train and mentor that underperformer. But if the underperformer continually fails to meet standards, then a leader who exercises Extreme Ownership must be loyal to the team and the mission above any individual. If underperformers cannot improve, the leader must make the tough call to terminate them and hire others who can get the job done. It is all on the leader.

This is a powerful lesson. It forms the foundation for leadership principles going forward.

Sometimes a leader asks, *Is it me, or is it them?*

When life at the office is rocky and not going the way you want, leaders often look at the team and ask, *Why can't I get them to perform the way I want them to?*

You might ask, *Do I just have unwilling people? Do they lack the ability to grasp the concepts and learn what to do? Are they lazy, rebellious, stupid, complacent, unmotivated, and unwilling?*

When the team is not moving in the right direction or not performing at high levels, the wise leader will consider his or her own role in the team's performance.

A Personal Example of This Concept from My Own Life

Let me share an example of this leadership concept from my own life.

For years I sponsored classes and training for our team of massage therapists. The classes focused on therapeutic-level massage, the type of bodywork where the therapist attempts to correct a client's specific

47

Leadership: Building and Nurturing a World-Class Team of Massage Therapists

problem. I trained therapists on topics such as neck pain, headaches, TMJ pain, low back pain, and dozens of other muscle-based problems.

I held these classes for years at a tremendous cost to the company that eventually reached $500,000 per year.

But there was a problem.

Through a series of events, it became painfully obvious that most of the therapists who went through the training were not doing advanced-level work. They were simply giving their clients a nice massage and saying, "I hope this helps." Then they would move on to the next client. For several years, I caught glimpses of what was going on. Then I started talking with the therapists. I asked some of them, "Why aren't the therapists doing this work?"

Often, the responses from fellow therapists went something like this:

- "The therapists are lazy."
- "The work is too hard."
- "The therapists don't want to do this work."
- "The therapists don't really care."

Nearly all the feedback I received placed the blame on the therapists. It was them. This went on for six or seven years.

For years, I kept asking myself, "How can we teach this more effectively? What am I not communicating about this work that keeps people unmotivated to actually do the work?"

Actually, this was not the therapists' fault. It was a failure on my part. I was convinced I was still not properly teaching and communicating the value of the work.

I kept revising our training methods. For years I attempted to give more precise instructions, and over time, we did make progress. But in early 2018, a series of events convinced me we still were not impacting therapists and clients to a high degree with this important work. Again, I started to ask the therapists why.

Section 3: Extreme Ownership

Why were the therapists still not generally doing this work?

They were taking classes.

They told us they loved the work.

They said they saw the value of the work.

But they still were not using the techniques to treat their clients. They were still doing basic standard massage techniques for complicated, severe pain patterns. And the customers were not getting the relief they were seeking. I continued for months to ask questions and ponder this situation. What was I missing? What was wrong with our training?

People kept telling me it wasn't the training; it was the therapists. But I wouldn't accept that answer. There must be something I was *still* not doing right.

A few training ideas eventually surfaced, and then more and more ideas came. After a few months, I was ready to start a new class that would focus not on advanced bodywork techniques, but on the actual *implementation* of the methods. It has been two years since I started that new class, and it has been a game-changer. The course went from a couple of basic ideas to twelve hours of additional training. We are now teaching many important concepts related to the actual practice side of therapeutic level bodywork. I would have never developed that material if I had accepted the original reason that it was the therapists' fault.

[**Note:** Truth be known, there probably is a degree of blame to place on the therapists. The point here is that I can't control what therapists believe, think, or desire. I only have control over myself. Thankfully, I have kept my focus all these years on what *I* can do. I haven't blamed my lack of impact on things or people outside of myself.]

I share this story with you because when I read the book *Extreme Ownership*, I understood the idea that the leader must own everything in his or her world, there is no one else to blame. That was a powerful idea for me. I believed in this concept, and I refused to blame the therapists. I kept looking inside. I kept asking what I could do to change the results.

And I am so grateful I kept asking questions. After teaching these classes for thirteen years, I still had twelve hours of very important training inside my head. And that would have never come out if I had not kept asking myself *Why?*

Why are the therapists not successful with this material? What am I still missing?

A leader must own everything in this world; there's no one else to blame. I'm a big believer in this concept.

Some very well-respected leadership experts make a case that it's always the leader's fault if sufficient progress is not being made in an organization. It might be for no other reason than the leader has selected the wrong team members. But maybe those team members have not been trained properly.

Training is a leadership function.

Here's another key point: If it's not the leaders, then leaders are simply victims. They have no control, and there is little they can do. That creates a feeling of helplessness. But if it's the leaders' fault, then they can take action to improve the situation. They are not helpless victims. Seeing it as "a leadership problem" gives leaders the power to change what is happening. There is still a component of team member responsibility, but a good leader will see when the team needs help and then train or replace those team members. That throws the ultimate responsibility back on the leader.

This is not just a valuable lesson for business leaders; it's a very useful and powerful life lesson for everyone. Take responsibility for the results you get in life. Don't blame factors outside yourself. We give up our power to the extent we blame outside factors.

Be Clear to Others

Let's say a team leader understands this concept and believes it passionately. What about the team? Somehow, they need to learn the concept, understand it, and believe it, too. Kim Scott, author of the book *Radical Candor*, explains it well.

Section 3: Extreme Ownership

Make thoughts/ideas drop-dead easy for others to comprehend.
When I was at business school, one of my professors told a story about a meeting between President Franklin Delano Roosevelt and the economist John Maynard Keynes. FDR was enormously busy, but he spent well over an hour with this academic. If FDR had understood Keynesian economics, some think the Great Depression might have ended sooner and enormous suffering could have been prevented. But at the end of the meeting, the president was not persuaded.

My professor asked the question, "Whose fault was it? FDR's for not understanding, or Keynes's for not explaining it well?" This was one of those moments in my education that changed my life. I'd always shifted the burden of responsibility for understanding to the listener, not to the explainer. But now I saw that if Keynes's genius was locked inside his head, it may as well not have existed. It was his responsibility to make the ideas that seemed so obvious to him equally obvious to FDR. He failed. Far too often we assume that if somebody doesn't understand what we're telling them, it's because they are "stupid" or "closed-minded." That is very rarely the case. While we know our subject matter, we may fail to know the person to whom we are explaining the subject, and therefore may fail to get our idea across.

This is a crucial application for the concept of extreme ownership. When you are trying to communicate or teach a principle, it's the teacher's responsibility to get the ideas across so learning takes place. It's not the responsibility of the listener. This concept was useful as I sought input on the clarity of this book. When I asked for feedback, I was careful to explain that the reader should grasp the concepts and ideas I'm sharing. If the idea wasn't clear or the reader wondered what I was trying to say, then I had failed as a writer. I had to rewrite that section so the reader would understand it. It's my responsibility as the author to get the message out

51

clearly and understandably. It's not the reader's responsibility to be able to read my mind. That's what Kim Scott was saying in *Radical Candor* about the insightful lesson from her professor. In the meeting between FDR and John Maynard Keynes, Keynes failed to communicate effectively. Communicating the ideas in a clear, understandable way was his responsibility.

These are great lessons for leaders as we look at cultivating extreme ownership.

Core Leadership Concept #2

There are no bad teams, just bad leaders.

In *Extreme Ownership*, the authors describe a series of races that SEAL teams participated in as part of their initial training. Several groups competed in a series of intense, exhausting boat races that went on for several hours.

> (From *Extreme Ownership*)
> In every race, there were standout performers. Throughout this particular Hell Week, one boat crew dominated the competition: Boat Crew II. They won or nearly won every single race. They pushed themselves hard every time, working in unison and operating as a team. Boat Crew II had a strong leader, and each of the individual boat crew members seemed highly motivated and performed well...
>
> Meanwhile, Boat Crew VI was delivering a standout performance of a different kind. They placed dead last in virtually every race, often lagging far behind the rest of the class. Rather than working together as a team, the men were operating as individuals, furious and frustrated at their teammates. We heard them yelling and cursing at each other from some distance, accusing the others of not doing their part. Each boat crew member focused on his

Section 3: Extreme Ownership

own individual pain and discomfort, and the boat crew leader was no exception...

Our SEAL senior chief petty officer, the most experienced and highly respected noncommissioned officer of the SEAL instructor cadre, took a keen interest in Boat Crew VI and their lackluster leader.

"You had better take charge and square your boat away, sir," said Senior Chief to the Boat Crew VI leader... Now, Senior Chief offered an interesting solution to Boat Crew VI's atrocious performance.

"Let's swap out the boat crew leaders from the best and the worst crews and see what happens," said Senior Chief. All other controls would remain the same—heavy and awkward boats manned by the same exhausted crews, cold water, gritty and chafing sand, wearied men competing in challenging races. Only a single individual, the leader, would change.

Could it possibly make any difference? I wondered...

Having received the direction to swap places, each boat crew leader went to his new position in the opposite boat crew and stood by for the next race. As before, boat crew leaders were given instructions, and they in turn briefed their teams.

"Stand by ... bust 'em!" came the command. And they were off.

We watched the boat crews sprint over the berm carrying their boats, then hurry down to the surf zone and into the dark water. They jumped into their boats and paddled furiously... We could no longer see the boat numbers... A half mile down the beach, as the instructors' trucks followed, the boat crews paddled back into shore. As the boats came in on the headlights, the numbers were clearly visible. Boat Crew VI was in the lead and maintained first place all the way across the finish line, just ahead of Boat Crew II. Boat Crew VI had won the race.

53

Leadership: Building and Nurturing a World-Class Team of Massage Therapists

A miraculous turnaround had taken place: Boat Crew VI had gone from last place to first. The boat crew members had begun to work together as a team, and *won*. Boat Crew II still performed well, though they narrowly lost the race...

It was a shocking turn of events. Boat Crew VI, the same team in the same circumstances only under new leadership, went from the worst boat crew in the class to the best. Gone was their cursing and frustration. And gone too was the constant scrutiny and individual attention they had received from the SEAL instructor staff. Had I not witnessed this amazing transformation, I might have doubted it. But it was a glaring, undeniable example of one of the most fundamental and important truths at the heart of Extreme Ownership: there are no bad teams, only bad leaders.

How is it possible that switching a single individual—only the leader—had completely turned around the performance of an entire group? The answer: leadership is the single greatest factor in any team's performance. Whether a team succeeds or fails is all up to the leader. The leader's attitude sets the tone for the entire team. The leader drives performance—or doesn't.

This drives the lesson home. There are no bad teams, just bad leaders.

Core Leadership Concept #3
Good leaders don't make excuses.

(From *Extreme Ownership*)
"During my own training and performance in BUD/S as a boat crew leader," I told them, "I can remember many times when my boat crew struggled. It was easy to make excuses for our team's performance and why it wasn't what it should have been. But I learned that good leaders don't make excuses. Instead, they figure out a way to get it done and win.

Section 3: Extreme Ownership

It can be tempting to look for scapegoats, to look for reasons outside of yourself for why you are having difficulties. But good leaders don't make excuses. This leadership principle reminds us to look inward and resist blaming forces outside of ourselves.

Core Leadership Concept #4

Every team leader will make mistakes, and when that happens, the leader must confront those mistakes.

> (From *Extreme Ownership*)
> Every leader and every team at some point or time will fail and must confront that failure. That, too, is a big part of this book. We are by no means infallible leaders; no one is, no matter how experienced. Nor do we have all the answers; no leader does. We've made huge mistakes. Often, our mistakes provided the greatest lessons, humbled us, and enabled us to grow and become better. For leaders, the humility to admit and own mistakes and develop a plan to overcome them is essential to success. The best leaders are not driven by ego or personal agendas. They are simply focused on the mission and how best to accomplish it.

It is important for the leaders at Oak Haven Massage to create a culture where we not only tolerate failure, but we expect it. When mistakes happen, leaders should accept responsibility, review the lessons learned, and move on.

Core Leadership Concept #5

To be an effective leader in an organization, you must believe in the organization's mission and purpose.

> (From *Extreme Ownership*)
> When our SEALs in Task Unit Bruiser learned that they would be allowed to conduct combat operations only alongside Iraqi soldiers,

55

they were livid and completely against the idea. We knew the dangers in Ramadi from the enemy were already extremely high. There was no need to increase the risk to our force. Yet that is exactly what we were being directed to do. I didn't believe this mission made sense. I didn't believe it was smart. I didn't believe it would be successful. But as Task Unit Bruiser's commander, I knew my actions and mindset carried great weight among my troops. These were my orders, and for me to lead, I had to believe. So I kept my doubts to myself as I asked the simple question: Why? Why would the U.S. military leadership on the ground in Iraq and back in America—from Baghdad to the Pentagon to the White House—task Navy SEALs, other Special Operations, and U.S. Army and Marine Corps units with such a high-risk mission? I had seen how difficult combat could be with the best people by my side. Why make it harder? I knew I had to adjust my perspective, to mentally step back from the immediate fight just outside the wire and think about this question from a strategic level, as if I were one of those generals in Baghdad or back at the Pentagon. Sure, they were far from the front lines, but certainly, they had the same goal we did: to win. That led to another question: What was winning? It certainly wasn't winning in the traditional military sense of the word. There would be no surrender from this enemy we fought against. There would be no peace treaty signed. Winning here meant only that Iraq would become a relatively secure and stable country. So I asked myself: How can we prepare the Iraqi soldiers to handle security in their own country? They needed to start somewhere. If there wasn't time to train Iraqi soldiers off the battlefield in a secure environment on base, then they would have to learn by doing, through OJT (on the job training). If the Iraqis never reached a level of skill at which they could defend their country from terrorist insurgents, then who would defend it? The answer was all too clear: us, the U.S. military. We would be stuck here securing their

Section 3: Extreme Ownership

country for them for generations. For those of us on the front lines of this conflict, it was clear that there were many senior U.S. military officers who, far removed from direct interaction with Iraqi soldiers, did not understand the Iraqi Army's true lack of capability. They were simply terrible, and no amount of training would make them excellent soldiers; but perhaps we could make them good enough. They could be good enough to handle a less substantial enemy. We could ensure the current enemy fit into that category by reducing the insurgents' ability to wage war. In addition to building the Iraqi Army's capability through training and combat-advising on the battlefield, we (our SEALs and U.S. forces) would have to crush the insurgency and lower its capability to a point where Iraqi soldiers and police would at least have a chance to maintain a relative peace by themselves—a chance to win. In order to do that, our Task Unit Bruiser SEALs needed to get outside the wire, onto the battlefield, and inflict serious damage on insurgent fighters. But we couldn't operate unless our combat missions received approval through our chain of command. The SEAL task unit that had been in Ramadi for the months prior to our arrival had told us they planned a number of combat operations consisting of only SEALs—without Iraqi soldiers. Almost all of those operations had been denied approval. In order to receive approval, I knew we must take Iraqi soldiers with us on every operation. They were our ticket to leave the base, push into enemy territory, and unleash fury upon the insurgents. With that, I understood, and I believed. Now, I had to ensure my troops understood and believed. The consensus from our SEALs, the frontline troops who would execute our missions, was clear: "This is garbage." I cut the not-so-subtle protest short: "I understand. The battlefield here in Ramadi is dangerous. It's difficult. Why make it even harder by forcing us to fight alongside Iraqi soldiers?" Damn right, nodded much of the room in agreement. "Well, let me ask you something," I

57

Leadership: Building and Nurturing a World-Class Team of Massage Therapists

continued. "If the Iraqi military can't get to a point where they can handle security in their own country, who is going to do it?" The room fell silent. I had their attention, and they knew the answer. But to ensure everyone clearly understood the strategic importance of why we were being directed to do this, I made it perfectly clear: "If Iraqi soldiers can't do it, there is only one group that will—us. The U.S. military will be stuck here for generations." I could see that, although there was still resistance to the idea of working with Iraqi soldiers, they were beginning to see this mission from a strategic perspective. "When the enemy is beaten, then the Iraqi Army can take over security duties for themselves." I saw some heads nod in agreement. "But to do that," I said, "we have to get each mission—each operation—approved. And if we want our missions approved, we must have Iraqi soldiers with us on every operation. Does anyone not understand this?" The room was quiet. Everyone understood. They didn't have to jump for joy at the thought of fighting alongside Iraqi soldiers on a dangerous battlefield. But they did have to understand why they were doing it so they could believe in the mission. Afterward, I spoke to my key leaders in greater detail about why this mission was important. "This place is on a downward spiral. We've got to do something different if we want to win. Every one of your operations will have Iraqi soldiers," I told them. "These Iraqi soldiers are our means to do something different—our ticket to operate. We will get them up to speed. We will prepare them the best we can. We will fight alongside them. And we will crush the enemy until even the Iraqi Army will be able to fight them on their own. Any other questions?" There were no more questions. The most important question had been answered: Why? Once I analyzed the mission and understood for myself that critical piece of information, I could then believe in the mission. If I didn't believe in it, there was no way I could possibly convince the SEALs in my task unit to believe in it. If

Section 3: Extreme Ownership

I expressed doubts or openly questioned the wisdom of this plan in front of the troops, their derision toward the mission would increase exponentially. They would never believe in it. As a result, they would never commit to it, and it would fail. But once I understood and believed, I then passed that understanding and belief on, clearly and succinctly, to my troops so they believed in it themselves. When they understood why, they would commit to the mission, persevere through the inevitable challenges in store, and accomplish the task set before us.

To convince and inspire others to follow and accomplish a mission, a leader must be a true believer in the mission. Once a leader believes in the mission, that belief shines through to those below and above in the chain of command. Your actions and words will communicate to the team whether you believe in the mission or not. With respect to the Oak Haven Massage mission:

- Do you believe we can enhance the lives of clients, team members, and shareholders?
- Do you believe the greatest rewards from involvement in a business might be not what you get from it, but what you become from your involvement with it?

Ask questions until you understand the mission. Do what is necessary so you can believe in what you are doing and can pass that information down the chain of command to your team with confidence. That is leadership.

Core Leadership Concept #6
It's crucial to lead both up and down the chain of command.

(From *Extreme Ownership*)
If your boss isn't making a decision promptly or providing necessary support for you and your team, don't blame the boss. First,

Leadership: Building and Nurturing a World-Class Team of Massage Therapists

blame yourself. Examine what you can do to better convey the critical information for decisions and support allocated. Leading up the chain of command requires tactful engagement with the immediate boss (or, in military terms, higher headquarters) to obtain the necessary decisions and support to enable your team to accomplish its mission and ultimately win. To do this, a leader must push situational awareness up the chain of command. Leading up the chain takes much more savvy and skill than leading down the chain. Leading up, the leader cannot fall back on his or her positional authority. Instead, the subordinate leader must use influence, experience, knowledge, communication, and maintain the highest professionalism. While it's essential to make your superior understand what you need, it's also important to realize that your boss must allocate limited assets and make decisions with the bigger picture in mind. You and your team may not represent the priority effort at that particular time. Or perhaps the senior leadership has chosen a different direction. Have the humility to understand and accept this. One of the most important jobs of any leader is to support your own boss—your immediate leadership. In any chain of command, the leadership must always present a united front to the troops. A public display of discontent or disagreement with the chain of command undermines leaders' authority at all levels. This is catastrophic to the performance of any organization. As a leader, if you don't understand why decisions are being made, requests denied, or support allocated elsewhere, you must ask those questions up the chain. Then, once understood, you can pass that understanding down to your team. Leaders in any chain of command will not always agree. At the end of the day, once the debate on a particular course of action is over, and the boss has made a decision—even if that decision is one you argued against— you must execute the plan as if it were your own.

60

Section 3: Extreme Ownership

When leading up the chain of command, use caution and respect. But remember, if your leader is not giving the support you need, don't blame him or her. Instead, reexamine what you can do to better clarify, educate, influence, or convince that person to give you what you need to win. The major factors to be aware of when leading up and down the chain of command are:

- Take responsibility for leading everyone in your world, subordinates and superiors alike.
- If someone isn't doing what you want or need them to do, look in the mirror first and determine what you can do to better enable this.
- Don't ask your leader what you should do, tell them what you are going to do.

Core Leadership Concept #7

As team leaders, we should train junior leaders and then allow them to do their job. The goal of a leader should be to work themselves out of a job.

One key responsibility of a leader and manager is to train and develop those we lead. There are many reasons to train those under our direction.

1. People want to grow. If we are not training and developing people, they will move on from our company.
2. Training and developing people is a key component of who Oak Haven Massage is. It's what's in our DNA.
3. We need a constant supply of new leaders to fill business needs as the company grows and as current team members move on to other opportunities.
4. Suppose a leader does not train team members who can move up the ranks and eventually move into the current manager's position. In that case, the current manager will never be allowed to leave their post.

61

Leadership: Building and Nurturing a World-Class Team of Massage Therapists

Training people under you to be able to take over your position seems a little scary. But if you think about it, that is the only way you will ever be able to move on to a new job with greater levels of responsibility and pay.

There is no place for a manager who is afraid to train people below him in a healthy organization due to fear they will take over their position.

Core Leadership Concept #8
Be close with the team but not too close.

(From *Extreme Ownership*)

A leader must be close with subordinates but not too close. The best leaders understand their team members' motivations and know their people—their lives and their families. But a leader must never grow so close to subordinates that one member of the team becomes more important than another, or more important than the mission itself. Leaders must never get so close that the team forgets who is in charge.

It's possible to get too close to members of the team you're leading. There are several problems that may arise when you do so. One is that the team may see closeness to one team member as favoritism or partiality. That may lead to negative feelings among the group members.

Another problem is that it may be more challenging to do your job as a manager when you have become friends with the team members. I'm referring here to the possibility that you may find it difficult to have the tough conversations required of a manager. That's especially true if a team member who is now your friend is not pulling his or her weight or misbehaving in some way.

These 8 Core Concepts are principles we come back to again and again every day in business. These concepts form the foundation of our leadership philosophy at Oak Haven Massage.

SECTION 4

General Leadership Principles

LET'S PUT LEADERSHIP IN PERSPECTIVE. WHAT MAKES SOMEONE A leader? Brené Brown defines leadership as "anyone who takes responsibility for finding the potential in people and processes, and who has the courage to develop that potential."[8]

John Wooden phrased it this way: *"A leader has a simple mission: to get those under his or her supervision to work at their highest level of ability in ways that best serve the team."*[9]

As a leader and manager, you are charged with finding the potential in business processes and in the people under your direction. Your task is to help the business fulfill its mission and vision. You're also tasked with helping your team achieve its goals, dreams, and desires.

Here are the primary tasks of an effective manager:

1. **Build culture** – create the environment, share the mission, discourage conflict, and promote honest communication.

---

8 "20 of the Best Leadership Quotes from Brené Brown," *CEO Magazine*, https://www.theceomagazine.com/business/management-leadership/20-of-the-best-leadership-quotes-from-brene-brown/

9 John Wooden, and Steve Jamison, *Coach Wooden's Leadership Game Plan for Success*, New York: McGraw-Hill, 2009, 134–135.

2. **Build and develop a high-functioning team** – attract, hire, onboard, develop, and retain.

3. **Develop and improve business processes** – serve clients' needs, make a profit.

This section will cover a wide range of leadership and management philosophies, principles, guidelines, and skills you will need daily to accomplish the three primary tasks of an effective manager.

Never Forget—People Come First

Sometimes we forget we are ultimately in the people business. People come before anything else. Kim Scott, in her excellent book *Radical Candor*, tells the following story and teaches an important lesson for managers.

Scott had just arrived at work with her new start-up company. She had all kinds of important jobs to do that day. As she walked into the building, her head was racing with a list of essential items.

> I had gotten only a few steps into the office when a colleague suddenly ran up. He needed to talk right away. He had just learned he might need a kidney transplant, and he was completely freaked out. After an hour and two cups of tea, he seemed calmer.
>
> I walked towards my desk, past an engineer whose child was in the ICU. "How did your son do last night?" I asked. He hadn't improved. As he told me how the night had gone, we both had tears in our eyes. I convinced him to leave the office and go take care of himself for an hour before returning to the hospital.
>
> I left his desk drained, passing by our quality assurance manager. His child had better news; she had just received the highest score in the entire state on a standardized math test. He wanted to talk about it. I felt emotional whiplash as I jumped from sympathy to celebration.

Section 4: General Leadership Principles

By the time I got back to my desk, I had no time or emotional reserves to think about the pricing problem I had started my day thinking about. I cared about each of these people, but I also felt worn out and frustrated that I couldn't get any "real" work done. Later that day, I called my CEO coach Leslie Koch to complain.

"Is it my job to build a great company?" I asked. "Or am I really just some sort of emotional babysitter?"

Leslie, a fiercely opinionated ex-Microsoft executive, could barely contain herself. "This is not babysitting!" she said. "It's called management, and it is your job!"

Whenever I feel I have something more important to do than listen to people, I remember Leslie's words. "It's your job!"

I have used Leslie's line on dozens of new managers who come to me after a few weeks in their new role, complaining that they feel like "babysitters" or "shrinks."

We undervalue the emotional labor of being the boss. Being a boss is hard emotional work. This emotional labor is not just part of the job; it's the key to being a great boss.

Care About People

The best and most influential managers care about people. As the saying goes, "People don't care how much you know until they know how much you care."

Take an interest in your team. Learn about their family, their interests, and their dreams. Know them on a personal level, not simply a professional level.

It's vital that you not only care, but that your team knows you care by the way you act.

65

Leadership: Building and Nurturing a World-Class Team of Massage Therapists

Keep an Emotional Bank Account

Think of your relationship with your team the same way you think of a bank account. We all know that before we can make a withdrawal from a bank account, we must first make a deposit. If the withdrawals outpace the deposits, we have an overdrawn account.

We can compare our interactions with our team members with that bank account. Take care to make more deposits in your emotional bank account—praise, care, concern, teaching—than you ever make in withdrawals—criticism, negative or corrective feedback, reprimands.

Here are some other ways to make deposits:

- Keep commitments
- Clarify expectations
- Show personal integrity
- Apologize sincerely—excuse-free apologies when you make a mistake

Build Trust

It's difficult to build a business without trust. In fact, building trust is one of the primary purposes of a business. Think about an advertisement for your business. It doesn't matter whether it's a print ad in a magazine or newspaper, a radio ad, or a social media ad on Facebook. Chances are, that ad is making a promise to a potential customer—something like this:

Best massage ever. Come try us out...only $65

Most ads promise the customer something. The above ad is no exception. It promises the "best massage ever." But it could have promised any number of things. It could have offered the best service, an awesome guarantee, quick delivery, or the best selection. It could have offered something that will change your life. The promise can be anything.

66

Section 4: General Leadership Principles

It's been said that the purpose of a business is to make a nearly unbelievable promise to a customer and then gear your entire business toward fulfilling that promise.

That is how I see business—making and keeping promises. We make promises to the customer, the team, and the shareholders (investors, owners).

With this as a background, a manager's job (or one of a manager's many jobs) is to nurture and build trust with the customers, the team, and the shareholders. I will go so far as to say that *it's impossible to build a great business without trust.* Trust flows in all directions in a fully functioning company.

Employees trust management.

Customers trust the company.

Shareholders trust management.

When I opened our first office in Austin, I learned firsthand the challenge of managing a business where trust was lacking. There was a very low level of trust among the initial team we assembled. Evidently, these people had former employers and bosses who had proven to be untrustworthy. Many of them shared the difficult times they had with former employers. They were hesitant to trust anyone in a management position. As the owner, I was lumped into a group that included all the people they had collectively known and mistrusted in the industry. As far as they were concerned, I could also not be trusted. I was not accustomed to that. I had been in business for more than 22 years, and I had always enjoyed a good relationship with the people who worked with me.

But this group did not trust me. They let me know in subtle ways that they didn't believe what I was saying. They did not trust me to fulfill any of the commitments I made. It was terrible. Over several years, I gradually earned the staff's trust. It was a slow and challenging process. I feel like I now have the confidence of the team in Austin. But I will never forget how it felt and what it was like to not have that trust.

67

Leadership: Building and Nurturing a World-Class Team of Massage Therapists

What Is Trust?

Trust is a leap we make. Trust is an assumption we make about a person's motives, character, ability, or actions. To trust someone is to rely on them. Trust can be thought of as a feeling or a hunch about someone or something.

What allows us to make this leap of trust? There must be a basis for trust. Something foundational must be present in order for trust to be established.

The foundation for trust is made up of these four interwoven components:

1. Motives or intent
2. Character
3. Ability
4. Actions

Motives or Intent

When we interact with people, we are continually judging (even if it's subconscious) what the person's intent or motive is.

> Trust begins to emerge when we have a sense that another person or organization is driven by things other than their own self-gain.
>
> —Simon Sinek

What motivates people's actions toward us? Are their motives honorable? Do they mean us harm? Are they seeking our greatest good? Or are they acting out of self-interest? At the heart of distrust is suspicion about a person's motives, which are rarely known by those on the outside. Unless the person is telling us what their motives are, we can only guess.

Sometimes we perceive a combination of self-interest and our interest. If we think there is a mixture, which there almost always is, we must decide to what degree the interaction is skewed toward them and to what degree toward us. We are continuously evaluating a person's motives and intent as we ask ourselves, "Are they worthy of our trust?"

Section 4: General Leadership Principles

Character

Character is another foundational component of trust. An entire book could be written on character, but we will give you a quick overview and summary here. For our purposes, let's consider character a combination of *ethics* and *authenticity*.

- **Ethics** – A person is ethical to the degree they have a system of moral principles that guide them. We might say they have specific internal rules of conduct. These rules of conduct generally include honesty. Someone is honest when they have honorable intentions and actions.
- **Authenticity** – Authenticity is representing ourselves accurately and honestly. It's being willing to show who we really are versus a made-up version of ourselves. Authenticity means we are being real. It's a what-you-see-is-what-you-get representation of us. When we are inauthentic, we are fake or false. When we are authentic, we are acting genuinely and sincerely.

Ability

Another basis for trust is the level of confidence in the abilities of a person we are dealing with. Someone can be very honest, have a strong character, and exhibit pure motives but not know what they are talking about in a specific area. Their lack of competence, ability, or knowledge in an area may lead to a lack of trust. To trust a person in a specific area, we must be sure they have the skill set and the knowledge base to function adequately in that area. Otherwise, our trust level is low.

Actions

From an evolutionary standpoint, people have a built-in need to judge trustworthiness—and to do it fast. Their survival may be at stake. They watch a person's actions and quickly make a decision about their level of

69

reliability. That's all people really have to go on since they intuitively know they cannot rely on a person's words alone. Words are important, but only in the context of congruence—the matching of actions to words.

It takes the following four components for us to have high levels of trust:

1. Pure motives or intent
2. Strong character
3. High levels of competence or ability
4. Congruent actions

They factor into our willingness to trust someone. But they may not all factor in equally. In some cases, motives will weigh in more. In other situations, character or competence will be more critical.

- **Even small actions matter** – What would you think of a leader whose secretary received a sales call from someone, and the leader told the secretary to tell the salesman he was not there? Or what if the leader told the secretary to say he was in a meeting when he was not? How do you think this leader's actions will affect his credibility and trust with his team? Even little white lies that are seemingly harmless can destroy trust. The only way a leader can build trust is by being trustworthy.
- **Actions that create trust** – Building trust happens with your team in small increments, bit by bit, over time, as you take action. Actions are powerful. They can build up or destroy trust. Here are some actions that will build trust in the organization. Remember, the process of building trust in an organization starts with the leader.
  - Do what you say you will do. Keep your commitments.
  - Show that you care for more than just your own interest. Seek a win-win. Look out for the welfare of your team and those you are doing business with.

70

Section 4: General Leadership Principles

- Demonstrate humility, not know-it-all arrogance. Admit mistakes.
- Treat others with respect and dignity, even when no one is watching.
- Be transparent, clear, and truthful, even when it's difficult.
- Give credit to others. Give credit where credit is due.
- Speak well of others. Speak of others as if they were in the room. Speaking ill of others when they are not present will erode trust. Have a strict no-gossiping policy for yourself.
- Trust your team members. Extend trust even before it is earned. People will stay with companies that trust them and give them the freedom to make decisions. They will leave companies where trust is low. It's not a good feeling to think your boss or your company does not trust you.

The Price of Openness

Leaders often have what they think are legitimate reasons for not being completely open and honest with their team. Let's face it, there can be a price to pay for an honest, open style. In Section 5, we explore honest conversations in detail. For now, we'll look at a few reasons why it can be difficult to be completely honest and open with your team.

- **Fear of consequences** – Leaders are less than honest for a reason. It might seem easier to give a fabricated, dishonest answer than the hard truth. If you fear the repercussions of a decision, you might skip the truth to avoid the consequence. The problem with the easy way out is that you are often found out, and your credibility and reputation suffer. You can work for years to establish credibility and trust and then destroy it in an instant. Should that happen, it can be exceedingly difficult or impossible to get it back.

Leadership: Building and Nurturing a World-Class Team of Massage Therapists

- **Fear of hurting another's feelings** – Sometimes the truth hurts. There's no denying that the truth can cause hard feelings. But it's better to have a small hurt feeling than to lie in an attempt to soften the blow. The risk of softness is a damaged reputation.
- **Fear of confrontation** – Telling the truth can be confrontational. You can often avoid direct conflict with a false statement. Sometimes it works. But when it doesn't... You'd better just bite the bullet and confront. No one said this leadership thing was easy. No one ever said building trust was the easy way out. It's often the more difficult path, especially in the short term. In the long term, it most definitely is the superior path.
- **Fear of how you will be perceived** – This is related to the desire for popularity or the need to be liked. It's challenging to be honest and open as a leader. You will need to make hard decisions. Some of those decisions will not be popular. Some of them will make people upset or angry with you. If your main concern is how you are perceived or if your priority is being popular, then leadership and management might not be your cup of tea.
- **Lack of courage** – It takes courage to do the right thing.
- Trust is an essential quality for a manager and a leader. Developing trust is one of your primary responsibilities and also one of your most challenging tasks. It's a virtue that is well worth cultivating in your role as a leader.

Navigate the Whirlwind

In business, the word *whirlwind* describes the craziness of a manager's day-to-day life. From the moment you step in the door at work, it's go here and go there. Got a minute? Problem here...problem there. All...Day...Long.

The whirlwind is taxing, unyielding, exhausting, and unrelenting. If we are wise, we see it as the detractor it is. If we're not careful, we can let our self-image get wrapped up in the whirlwind. We can become addicted to

Section 4: General Leadership Principles

how important we feel when everyone needs us. It feeds our ego to think that the place can't get along without us. The whirlwind keeps us from doing our most important work and forces us to work on the task that screams the loudest. The whirlwind wants us to spend time on the urgent.

It's critical to take time to decide what your most important work is. It's essential to determine what areas of the business need your attention and how you can move projects forward. The whirlwind wants to decide for us. Urgency beckons at every turn. If you are not careful, you can let urgency choose where you spend your time and energy. The whirlwind never stops and is unyielding. How do you escape its influence?

Stepping out of the whirlwind starts with believing it's possible. Overcoming the whirlwind begins with commitment. You must commit to yourself to spend your time on the issues that matter and not reacting to problems and urgencies.

There is a way out of the whirlwind. You must think, strategize, plan, organize, and train your way out of the whirlwind, and you must believe that your efforts to escape will be worth the struggle.

Seth Godin seems to understand the challenges of the whirlwind.

> "There's a common safe place: Being busy.
>
> We're supposed to give you a pass because you were full on, all day. Frantically moving from one thing to the other, never pausing to catch your breath, and now you're exhausted.
>
> No points for busy.
>
> Points for successful prioritization. Points for efficiency and productivity. Points for doing work that matters.
>
> No points for busy."

Leadership: Building and Nurturing a World-Class Team of Massage Therapists

How do you fight the whirlwind and make sure your days are spent working on the important and not only the urgent?

You prioritize.

You ask yourself, "What is most important?"

Stephen Covey's Important, Urgent Quadrant

Stephen Covey shared the graphic below in his book *The 7 Habits of Highly Effective People.* It illustrates the concept that urgent matters come in two forms: urgent and not urgent. An example of Quadrant I might be the bathroom is overflowing with water. It's both important and urgent. An example of Quadrant II might be developing a yearly marketing plan. It's important, but no one is screaming about it. An example of Quadrant III might be the phone ringing with a sales call on the other end. And an example of Quadrant IV could be a friend request on Facebook.

	URGENT	NOT URGENT
IMPORTANT	**Quadrant I** urgent and important **DO**	**Quadrant II** not urgent but important **PLAN**
NOT IMPORTANT	**Quadrant III** urgent but not important **DELEGATE**	**Quadrant IV** not urgent and not important **ELIMINATE**

Section 4: General Leadership Principles

Urgent things drive our attention and will get taken care of by virtue of their urgency. It's the not urgent issues that are still important that we need to pay attention to. We might delay working on these issues for weeks, months, or years because they are not urgent. It's a great practice to look at the important, not urgent, items on our list and make time for them.

Knowing your priorities is an important first step, but you must also look at the systems and processes that will get you out of the whirlwind. Just putting out the fire is not enough. You have to look at the root of the problem and see if there is a solution that would prevent that problem from reoccurring.

Gary Keller's amazing book, *The One Thing,* has this brilliant thesis: "If you wish to maximize your value to the company, you must spend your time working on the most important items. And you should spend no time on less important items."[10]

What are those important items? That's the challenge for you to decide. Of all the things you could do, what is *the one thing* you must do to have maximum impact?

> There can be one most important thing. Many things may be important, but only one can be the most important.[11]

If you find out what the most important thing is and do it, you are doing the best service possible for the team and for the business.

Here's why finding that one thing is difficult:

> The things which are most important don't always scream the loudest.
>
> —Bob Hawke

---

10 Gary Keller, *The One Thing,* Austin, TX: Bard Press, 2013, ____ .

11 Ross Garber, quoted in Keller, _____ .

It can be challenging to separate the urgencies of the whirlwind from the critical and very important. As Hawke's quote states, important stuff usually does not scream. This is another variation of Covey's concept of important and urgent quadrants.

Keller brings a favorite law into the discussion called the Pareto Principle.

> "Pareto's principle, it turns out, is as real as the law of gravity, and yet most people fail to see the gravity of it. It's not just a theory—it is a provable, predictable certainty of nature and one of the greatest productivity truths ever discovered. Richard Koch, in his book *The 80/20 Principle*, defined it about as well as anyone: 'The 80/20 principle asserts that a minority of causes, inputs, or efforts usually lead to a majority of the results, outputs, or rewards.'"[12]

Keller mentions Koch's principle to make his point that there are a few things done well (the 20 percent) that will give you results and impact far beyond the effort expended. The Pareto Principle is real proof that not all things matter equally. Some things matter more—much more. And it's worth your time to figure out what those things are.

The To-Do List

Keller cautions us against the evils of the to-do list. Don't worry about the list, he advises; worry about finding the one thing on the list.

> "No matter how many to-do's you have, you can always narrow it down to one. Once you figure out what matters, keep asking what matters most until there is only one thing left. That core activity goes at the top of your success list.

---

12 Keller, _____ .

Section 4: General Leadership Principles

Don't get trapped by the "check it off" game. Not all things matter equally, and we must act accordingly."

Stay on Task

Once you find the one thing, the challenge shifts. Your challenge now becomes staying on task and avoiding multitasking.

"Staying on task is critical. Researchers estimate that workers are interrupted every eleven minutes and then spend almost one-third of their day recovering from these interruptions. If we really lose nearly one-third of our workday to distractions, what is the cumulative loss over a career?

"We know that multitasking can even be fatal in some professions. We fully expect pilots and surgeons to focus on their jobs to the exclusion of everything else. And we hope that anyone in their position who gets caught doing otherwise will always be taken to task. We accept no arguments and have no tolerance for anything but total concentration from professionals. Yet, here are the rest of us, living another standard. Do we not value our own job or take it seriously? Why would we ever tolerate multitasking when we're doing our most important work? Just because our day job doesn't involve bypass surgery shouldn't make focus any less critical to our success. Our work deserves no less respect."

Be like a postage stamp. Stick to one thing until you get there.

—Josh Billings

Leadership: Building and Nurturing a World-Class Team of Massage Therapists

Part of Staying on Task is the Ability to Say No

"Say 'no' or 'not now' to anything else you could do until your most important work is done. People would be amazed to know how many things **do not** need to be done.

Until your one thing is done, everything else is just a distraction."

"Focus is a matter of deciding what things you're **not** going to do."

—John Carmack

Sometimes it's your boss you must learn to say no to. If you have a boss who is continually giving you projects, adding to an already full plate, here is a way to let them know you are at your max. When they ask you to take on another project, open your weekly planner or some other document where you keep all your priorities and say, "I'm happy to take on this project; which of these would you like me to set aside so I will have the bandwidth for this?"

On Learning to Say No

Seth Godin says, "you can say no with respect, you can say no promptly, and you can say no with a referral to someone who might say yes. But saying yes, because you can't bear the short-term pain of saying no, is not going to help you do the work."

Sometimes, when we are very busy, we can fool ourselves into thinking we have been productive the entire day. Keller makes a distinction between busy and productive: don't focus on being busy; focus on being productive. Allow what matters most to drive your day.

Section 4: General Leadership Principles

How Do We Focus on Our Most Important Task?

"Block your time in the morning. It's your most productive time. Although time blocking isn't hard, protecting the time you've blocked is. The world doesn't know your purpose or priorities and isn't responsible for them, you are. The best way to protect your time blocks is to adopt the mindset that they can't be moved."

It is tempting to let our email inbox dictate how we start and spend our day. While it is essential to monitor your inbox and respond to important emails timely, it is also not the best way to start your day. It can suck you in and keep you from accomplishing and working on your most important task. You should have time in your day allocated for emails, but consider not using your most productive time for that.

How to Delegate a Task or Project

If we, as managers and leaders, are going to spend our time working on only what matters, there will be a lot of items that we must pass along to our assistants and other department heads. We simply can't do everything. Our objective is to spend our time on **the one thing**.

So, let's talk about delegation. Here is how a manager might delegate a task or project.

Manager: Hey, would you mind doing this for me?

Team member: Sure, no problem.

Manager: Thank you, I really appreciate it.

Let's look at a second example of a manager asking for help with a task.

Manager: Hey, would you mind doing this for me?

Leadership: Building and Nurturing a World-Class Team of Massage Therapists

Team member: Sure, no problem.

Manager: Thank you, I really appreciate it. Is it possible to have it to me by this Friday?

Team member: Of course.

Manager: Great, will you follow up with me on Wednesday and give me a progress report? I'm here if you have any questions or you get stuck.

You will notice in the second request that the manager did a couple of things different. She set a due date. In the first example, the due date for the project was left open. When no due date is mentioned, the person receiving the assignment assumes it's expected when they have time for it. This is a sure-fire way for misunderstanding to lead to disappointment. Also, the second request set up a chance for an update midway through the timeframe. This will be helpful in keeping the assignment on track. The manager also made herself available in the second example for issues and questions should they arise. This way, the team member does not feel alone in the project. Whenever you delegate a task or assignment, it's good to have your vision for the project as clear as possible. If you can, and the project is significant enough, it will help to write up your requirements and specifications to the degree possible. If the project is large, it's helpful to have a brief check-in very early on. It's better to find out as early as possible if you have competing visions about what the finished product will look like.

Leadership and Dissatisfaction

It might surprise you to know that at the heart of a great leader is dissatisfaction. I'm not talking about a complete and total kind of dissatisfaction where the leader is depressed, pessimistic, and frustrated. I'm describing a healthy level of dissatisfaction where a leader has a level of contentment or happiness, combined with a general sense of gratitude. But underlying it all

Section 4: General Leadership Principles

is a healthy discontent with the status quo, an unrelenting need to look for ways to make things better. What if Henry Ford was content with his horse? What if Steve Jobs was happy and satisfied with his flip phone? What if Elon Musk was satisfied with his gas guzzling Suburban. The world moves forward on the back of the dissatisfied leader, looking for a better way.

I love what author Seth Godin had to say on this topic:

> "For those who seek mastery, for those who want to be the best, for those who want to leave mediocrity behind them, dissatisfaction is constantly with them. The dissatisfaction is fuel knowing that you can improve, realizing that you have an obligation to make things better. Everywhere you look, you see opportunities to improve. It's important to realize that it is possible to live with dissatisfaction while at the same time knowing that progress is ongoing. It doesn't have to be perfect tomorrow. It's a lifelong quest. We see what needs improvement, we seek Mastery, but we are patient knowing we may never quite get there."

It's important to nurture a healthy level of dissatisfaction. It's this "healthy dissatisfaction" that keeps leaders constantly looking for ways to improve. And what are we looking to improve?

Everything!

We want to improve everything from marketing to operations to culture. What's more is that we will never be satisfied with how things are. Grateful, yes; happy, yes; but never satisfied.

Generally speaking, most managers and most team members do not have this "restless discontent." It's relatively rare. Most team members, even great team members, will continue to check the boxes, answer the phones, greet the clients the way it's always been done. Most will have no thought to how it could be done better or how we could reduce the friction with customer experiences. Most team members will not contemplate how to make things cost less and give the customer a better experience in the process. Because it's so rare, if you as a manager cultivate this restless discontent with your team, it will separate you from the crowd.

Lead and Inspire Innovation

We have talked about great leaders and their underlying tendency towards dissatisfaction. These leaders are the poster children for a growth mindset. They're always looking to improve everything. They want to improve themselves as well as the people around them. Business products and processes are also on their radar. They are always looking to improve and innovate in all aspects of the business. Hopefully, we won't be doing things the same way in two years as we are doing them now. What will change, and who will be the person or persons driving that change?

Great leaders inspire a level of dissatisfaction and desire for innovation among the teams they lead. This focus on innovation permeates the business culture. It becomes part of "how we do things around here." One of a leader's important jobs is to continually encourage and invite team members to look critically at all aspects of the products and services they offer.

- What could be different?
- How can we do it better, faster, cheaper with more profit and less waste?
- How can we reduce customer friction?
- How can we make it easier to do business with us?
- What do customers dislike about how we do things?
- Can we change those things?
- What do customers love about us?
- Can we do more of that?
- Where do we routinely miss it in regards to customer service?
- How can we structure our processes to fix those issues and solve those problems?

Section 4: General Leadership Principles

It would be wonderful if the entire team was involved in this quest to be better. Team members are on the "front lines." They are in the best position to see what is working and what is not. It's often the team member, not the leader, who is in the best position to change what is not optimal and find better ways to serve the customer. This topic of leading change is a never-ending task for a leader.

As a leader, inspire your team to find ways to do it better.

Fix the Problem, but Also Fix the Process

Where does innovation come from? How do we know what processes within the business are optimal, and which need tweaking or even total revamping? Clues for areas to retool business processes can come from many sources. I have a recommendation for one place to look for processes that might need improving. Look at problems.

Problems arise every day in business. Issues such as:

- The client was scheduled with the wrong therapist.
- The client claims they did not get their full allotted time.
- The client was taken back late.
- The therapist was late for the shift.

The list could go on and on. Managers are accustomed to dealing with and fixing problems. That's what they do. Next time a problem arises, rather than just fix the problem, take a good look at the problem. Was there something about the business process or the internal business system that allowed the situation to happen? Is there a way to not just fix the problem, but fix and alter the system that allowed the problem to occur in the first place? This thinking will potentially prevent future issues of this nature.

> Eighty-five percent of the reasons for failure are deficiencies in systems and processes rather than the employee.

Leadership: Building and Nurturing a World-Class Team of Massage Therapists

> The role of management should be to change the processes
> rather than badgering the people to do better.
>
> —W Edward Deming

This is a very valuable way for managers to teach themselves and their team to look at problems. Teach them to fix the problem, indeed. But look for the underlying process that allowed the situation to happen in the first place. Is there something in the process that needs correcting or tweaking?

One example of this is a few years ago, one of our managers was filling in at a different location. During her eight-hour shift, she saw three people get flustered and even upset at the fact that they were not notified that their massage would be in a different suite. At our Huebner location, we have an annex suite located just a few doors down from the main office. Clients would come to the main office to check-in, only to find out that their therapist was actually in the annex suite. Even though it is only about fifty steps to the other office, it is around the corner. If the client was running late or in a rush, even those extra fifty steps could be frustrating. The working manager saw people getting flustered and asked the other front desk team members if this was an ongoing problem. All of the heads nodded in agreement; they had seen people get frustrated for months and years, but everyone had just resigned themselves to the fact that "it is what it is."

They decided to text each client who would be in the annex the morning of their appointment to let them know they would need to go to a different suite. Virtually overnight, the problem went away. Clients were no longer frustrated, and the front desk didn't have to walk clients down or have anyone get upset with them.

Note to Leaders

With all this talk of "driving change," please note that not all team members will openly embrace change. In fact, you may encounter just the opposite. Many team members may resist change of any kind. The more significant

Section 4: General Leadership Principles

the change, the more resistance. It's a standard human characteristic to see change as threatening and to push back. I mention this not to discourage you, but in the spirit of full disclosure. Seek to inspire innovation, but be prepared for resistance.

This is important because sometimes, leadership sees clearly changes that need to happen. Leaders are sometimes surprised and saddened and even a bit shocked when team members are slow to embrace change that we see as being game changers.

Sometimes Innovation Fails

Not every new idea has a happy ending. Sometimes, despite our best effort, research, and planning, a new idea fails to have the impact we hoped. When this happens, it is important to admit failure, go back to the drawing board, and try again.

Last year, we were expanding and experiencing some growing pains with our payroll company. After months of research, interviewing, and planning, we launched a new payroll system. It was a disaster. People were not paid correctly, vacation time did not accrue properly, and did not sync properly with our insurance company. There was a slew of other issues as well.

We had planned for months, invested tens of thousands of dollars, and put in over 500 hours of manpower to successfully launch this platform. After three pay periods, just six weeks, we threw in the towel and went back to our old payroll provider with our tail between our legs. Luckily, the payroll company welcomed us back with open arms. We realized they had made some major changes in the six weeks we were gone that allowed us to accomplish almost all of our original goals.

We quickly recognized we had not made the right decision and made the tough call to revert back to the original payroll company. After announcing to the team that it had failed and we would be going back to our old system, many employees reached out and thanked us for being open and honest.

Leadership: Building and Nurturing a World-Class Team of Massage Therapists

They also thanked us for always trying to make things better, even though they don't always work out.

Two additional important notes about innovation: First, don't make too many changes at once. That can cause the team to become overwhelmed and frustrated. Change must be done slowly to make sure it sticks, and the team is on board and trained without feeling pulled in too many directions. Secondly, for a new idea to be given the highest chance of success, it is essential to get buy-in from key team members to help champion the new idea. For example, if it is a new process for massage therapists, present your idea to the instructors and get them to help support you and promote it. The more people you can get to help implement your idea, the better!

Business First

Before you became a leader and manager, you may have thought that your personal relationships with your co-workers took precedence over any allegiance you had to the business. You may have considered your friendships more important than any loyalty you felt towards the company. When you become a manager, it's possible that your loyalties need to change. A manager is being paid to put the needs and the interest of the business over any personal relationships you might have with co-workers. If a manager doesn't think that is possible, that is okay. They should just decline a management position. A manager may need to give difficult feedback to a team member. As a manager, you may need to discipline or even dismiss a team member who is not performing adequately. This team member might have been a friend. These personnel issues are a critical part of a manager's responsibility. If you don't think you are up to the task, by all means, don't become a manager. If a manager allows personal friendships to get in the way of doing what is right for the business and the team, they are negligent in their responsibilities.

Related to this principle is that a leader must give up the need for approval, or the need to be liked by the staff. You cannot be "one of the

Section 4: General Leadership Principles

guys" and be a leader and manager at the same time. There will always be a need for some level of separation.

Leadership Can be a Lonely Calling

The idea that leadership is a lonely position has come up briefly a couple of times in this book. It is a topic that definitely bears repeating. For a manager to function effectively in their position, there must be some distance between the manager and the team they are called to lead. This poses a significant challenge for some leaders. Upon becoming a manager, the relationship between former co-workers and the newly named manager will need to shift

As a leader, it will be important to not show favoritism to specific team members. Showing preference for one person or for one group within your team is a sure way to bring down morale. It isn't even enough to not show favoritism; the team cannot feel any extra attention given to friends. Be especially aware of this when scheduling, letting behavior slide, and making exceptions to the rules.

No Job is Beneath You

Humans are constantly sending messages to other humans. Some of these messages are in the form of words. Some messages we send are in a non-verbal form. Whether it's the words we use or the actions we take, we are always sending messages. Some of the most powerful and influential messages we send are indeed through our actions.

We tend to have this understanding that people can say anything. It's what they do that really shows what they believe.

With that as a bit of a background, I have a question for you. What messages are we sending to our team if there are tasks that need to be done, but the leader will not do them?

Does it communicate:

- The leader is too good for that task?
- That task is below the leader?
- We are not really a team, but a group of "higher ups" and "lower, sorry people"?

If we are really a team trying to accomplish an objective, should we not all, including the leader, be willing to do any task that will help move the mission forward?

Now, before you point out that this mindset flies in direct conflict with my recommendation for a manager to get out of the whirlwind, set priorities, and work on the one most important thing, it's the general attitude and mindset I'm talking about here. I'm talking about the *willingness* to do whatever is necessary. I'm suggesting that a leader develop the mindset that we are all a team, and we all work to get the job done.

It's not that a leader should sweep up the mess on the floor or do the laundry or clean the bathroom. But they should be willing to do any and every task. When we are not willing to do all tasks, it sends a troubling sign, a nonverbal signal, to your team. And it's a signal that works against creating a fully functional unit.

Be willing to do whatever is necessary to help with the operation of the business. For the thoughtful, humble leader, no job is below them.

Catch People Doing Something Right

Managers are fixers by their very nature. It's what they do. They are looking to improve everything: culture, people, and business processes. Managers know the great satisfaction that comes with improving things. It feels good to see a problem in one area of the business, to consider it, debate options, research, and test possible solutions.

The same satisfaction can be found in developing a team. There is a lot of fulfillment that comes with recruiting and developing members of the team. Helping them learn to serve the customers at a higher and higher

Section 4: General Leadership Principles

level. Assisting the team members to become more and more valuable to the business. Knowing that as they become more valuable to the business, they can be paid more. It's a win-win scenario.

As leaders, we are always looking to improve processes and develop team members. If we are not careful and self-reflecting, we can spend too much time correcting and improving and not enough time praising. Catching people doing something right is a skill and practice worth developing. You can spend too much time looking for problems and not nearly enough time finding something to praise. As with many of the items I'm sharing with you, I learned this lesson through my own experience.

Thankfully, this tendency to find problems was brought to my attention by one of our front office staff in Austin. Whenever I was around, I was pointing out things they were doing wrong or processes that were not optimal. Even though I think my heart was in the right place, it was still a problem. I was doing my best to help them become more valuable to the business. I was always looking for ways to reinforce previous training. I ultimately wanted them to be able to provide our clients with world-class service. All these motives were reasonable and commendable. But my tendency to find things to criticize still had an overall negative impact on the staff. No one wants to continually hear that they are doing it wrong. It becomes disheartening. Humans thrive on praise; they can feel demoralized with constant criticism. Researchers say that most humans will do well with significantly more praise than criticism. Studies show that 90 percent praise versus 10 percent negative is a workable ratio for most people.

One way to minimize the effects of negative corrective feedback is to do your corrections in a group of two or more people. This has the benefit of not singling people out for negative feedback, but has the downside of not being direct enough. When you are in a group, the person who needs the feedback may not recognize that it was meant for them. Nevertheless, a group meeting is often the best way to start with

Leadership: Building and Nurturing a World-Class Team of Massage Therapists

corrective feedback. You can always meet with the person privately if the group session doesn't work.

If you are in upper management, you may want to adopt the philosophy (as I have) that you never correct or give negative feedback to a staff member. I found that even a minimal amount of negative feedback by someone in the upper management levels will have a wildly disproportional negative effect on the team member.

I have looked at this phenomenon and thought about it quite a bit. I think it has to do with a couple of issues. First, because I'm removed from day-to-day management, I don't have rapport with the team member. I've put nothing into our relationship account. It's tough to try to make a withdrawal in that situation. Secondly, they don't want the only interaction with you to be negative; it's deflating to the team member. If I see issues that need to be addressed, I will make a note of the issue, then mention it to someone who has managerial responsibility for the team member. I will explain what I observed and allow them to deal with the feedback. I have found that this is a much better approach.

It's good to keep in mind that your interactions with staff should be 90 percent positive and only 10 percent negative or corrective.

Catch people doing stuff right, rather than catching them doing things wrong. It will create a much more pleasant work culture. And you will have a more significant impact on your team.

Criticism, Feedback, and Correction

Criticism

Criticism comes from a place of disapproval and the desire to inform a person of problems or faults. Its focus is usually on the negative, what we don't want. The end result of criticism is often deflation in the self-esteem of the person receiving it. Humans are generally not fond of criticism and will often find a way to reject it to preserve self-esteem.

Section 4: General Leadership Principles

Feedback

Feedback is a helpful suggestion. The person receiving the feedback may accept or reject it. Feedback is designed to help another person develop or improve. It is mainly informational and often comes without judgment or chastisement.

There are two broad categories of feedback.

- One is **unsolicited** feedback. This is feedback the person did not request. In a work setting, this can come from a manager or a coworker. Unsolicited feedback can be a mixed bag, depending entirely on the nature of the feedback itself, the manner in which it is given, and the mood or disposition of the person receiving the feedback. Unsolicited feedback should be carefully weighed for value by the person giving the feedback. It may land better if it comes from a supervisor rather than a colleague. The general rule for unsolicited feedback from a colleague is to be careful. It often does not go well. Coworkers often perceive it as thinly veiled criticism rather than uplifting feedback. Feedback is best received by any person when it is solicited.
- **Solicited** feedback is feedback someone has requested. It usually comes in the form of a mentor/mentee relationship, where there is a sort of understood contract that the mentor will give feedback on ways the mentee can improve, grow, and develop.

Correction

Feedback is often a suggestion that could be excepted or rejected. Correction in the work environment comes from a supervisor and is often much more than a mere suggestion. It's feedback too, but a unique kind of feedback. It is information coming back to you about behaviors, situations, and concerns the manager deems unacceptable and must be remedied. Corrections by managers are generally issues that must be fixed or changed, or serious consequences may result.

91

We Get What We Tolerate

You ask yourself the question, *Why does Brad always come to work late?*

Brad might tell you it's the traffic. He might say the kids needed some extra help this morning, or he might say the dog ran out the door just as he was leaving. Brad will always have a reason why he is late.

But the truth is, he is late because he can be. You, as the manager, tolerate his lateness. He has no consequences for arriving to work late.

This is an important life lesson. We get in life what we tolerate.

If we create a situation with our staff where there is no consequence for a specific behavior, that behavior will likely continue. If there are no consequences to poor performance, that becomes the standard. One of the many jobs a leader has is to enforce standards. Most behaviors with staff will continue as long as we continue to tolerate that behavior.

This principle was demonstrated very powerfully with a situation we found ourselves in at Oak Haven Massage. Several years ago, we started to get a large number of complaints from clients. Clients told us on feedback forms that they were not getting their full allotment of time for the massage. Therapists were routinely shorting the time they spent with clients by anywhere from five to ten minutes. Over a period of several months, these complaints became more and more common. The management team finally reached the conclusion that we had to do something. The situation had become intolerable.

We spent about four months trying to understand the problem and brainstorming solutions. After a series of advisory meetings with five to ten therapists, and after several manager meetings, we eventually came to some conclusions and proposed a solution.

Here is what we discovered:

- Therapists were shorting specific customer's time to make up time and get back on schedule.
- Therapists were needing to make up time because they were careless in managing their time with their clients. They were

Section 4: General Leadership Principles

starting sessions late or running over with some clients, causing them to start late with another client.

- To get back on schedule, they were cutting off specific clients early before their full hour session, so it didn't cut into their break time
- There was no incentive for the therapist not to do this. If a client complained, the business would discount the session for the client. If the client was agitated, we would possibly let them have the session for free.
- The client was satisfied.
- The therapist received their full pay for the hour, which meant they were satisfied.

Everyone was happy except the business. We determined that the therapists were choosing to short time because there were no consequences for doing so.

They did it because they could. We, as a business, were tolerating this behavior. We decided to change our approach with the therapists. We changed our policy regarding how we dealt with clients who lodged a complaint about not getting their full session.

Here's what we did:

- If a client complained of a shortened session, they would get a 50 percent discount.
- The first time this happened each year, the therapist would not be penalized. They would simply be told that they had a complaint of a shortened time.
- After the first complaint, if it happened again, the therapist would only be paid for a half-hour session.

This put the responsibility on the therapists. Now, there was a consequence for shorting a client's time. The result of this policy was remarkable. In the two months after establishing this new policy, our complaints of shortened sessions virtually went away. I wouldn't have believed it if I had

93

Leadership: Building and Nurturing a World-Class Team of Massage Therapists

not seen it with my own eyes. The complaints disappeared. All it took was establishing a policy where we held the therapists responsible.

We re-learned the lesson "you get what you tolerate." All we had to do was to stop accepting the behavior, and the problem went away.

Side note: It is worth mentioning that we do not like punitive policies as a leadership style in general. We would prefer to find a way to fix an issue in a more positive way, either by reward or other positive reinforcement, but sometimes, having a consequence can be the best way to deal with a particular issue.

Venting

Managers have different rules than everyone else. Managers have to be careful when venting. The words you use and the thoughts you communicate have a way of getting back to team members. Sometimes you might vent to a co-worker, thinking it's a private conversation. You would be surprised to know how often comments find a way back to the person you were venting about. Of course, it's acceptable and expected for a manager to become frustrated. Managers must realize they have to deal with frustrations differently when they are in a leadership position. Their actions and words have far-reaching implications.

Hypothetical question: Should the staff be able to tell when the leader is having a bad day?

Dating Team Members

Dating team members under your direct supervision is most likely a bad idea. Some companies have internal policies that forbid dating between a supervisor and a team member. Other companies simply discourage it. If the relationship goes south, as it often does, the business might be exposed to harassment type liabilities. At Oak Haven Massage, any romantic relationship with your direct report is against our policy.

94

SECTION 5

Build and Nurture a World-Class Team

Here is what the process of building and nurturing a world-class team looks like:

You've heard this before: People Come First. This is never truer than when you are building your team. It's about people first.

Gary Vee…To build, you need humans   https://vimeo.com/472598915
Bill Gates…It's about the people   https://vimeo.com/472597573

Jim Collins wrote about this philosophy in the monumental book *Good to Great*:

> "First Who, Then What—get the right people on the bus. Those who build great organizations make sure they have the right people on the bus before figuring out where to

drive the bus. They always think first about who and then about what or where. Great vision without great people is irrelevant. If you have the right people on the bus, the problem of how to motivate and manage people largely goes away. The right people don't need to be "fired up;" they will be self-motivated by the inner drive to produce the best results and to be part of creating something great. If you have the wrong people, no matter what you do, you *still* won't have a great company."

Attract Team Members

We are looking to attract talented, motivated, inspired superstars to our organization; we are not looking for someone to fill an empty chair.

A world-class team starts with standards. Develop a set of world-class standards for your team, and then work hard to find those who meet your criteria.

> Great companies don't hire skilled people and motivate them; they hire motivated people and inspire them. People are either motivated to be the best or they are not.
> —Simon Sinek

Our job as leaders is to find motivated people and give them something to believe in. It's essential to be selective and willing to put significant effort into finding the right team members. Let's stick to the standard we have set and avoid settling just for the sake of filling an open position.

Let's focus on attracting potential team members to Oak Haven with our mission, our culture, our vision, and, ultimately, our humanity.

To find the most compatible team members, let's fully describe what exactly we are looking for in a potential team member. A clear vision of

Section 5: Build and Nurture a World-Class Team

what type of person we want to join our group is a prerequisite for finding the right person.

How Do We Describe and Define Our Perfect Oak Haven Massage Team Member?

The perfect team member at Oak Haven massage would want to serve the customer at the highest possible level. The ideal team member would like to be part of a cohesive, powerful, collaborative team.

I would say the number one quality to be successful in customer service is the ability to care. Caring supersedes any other personal quality when it comes to dealing with clients. If you add to this a strong desire to serve others, you have a winning combination. Other attributes that are very important in the world of customer service are empathy and rapport. Empathy is the ability to relate to what the other person is feeling. Rapport is the ability to build a connection with customers.

Oak Haven has a culture of constant and never-ending improvement. We are looking for team members who share this passion and commitment. We want to continually improve as individuals, as a group, and as a business. Inherent in this continual improvement is the willingness to always be learning and growing.

In addition, teamwork is a vital part of what makes Oak Haven unique. We are looking for great team players. We want people who like collaboration and want to be part of a functioning team. It is also vital to identify prospective team members who have a tremendous dislike for gossip and drama between coworkers.

Hire Team Members

Hiring team members to match the company's vision and direction is one of the critical tasks of management. I wish I could tell you it's going to be easy; it is not. As the saying goes, "If it was easy, everyone would do it."

Holding out to hire the most compatible team members will test your resolve. It will test your commitment to build an outstanding team. Filling slots is relatively easy, but continuing to interview day after day while your current team is overtaxed and overworked is very challenging.

One of the problems with making good hires is that the interview process itself is so very … well … inexact.

Hiring is not a hard science; it is soft and mushy. Applicants can be so persuasive. Let's face it, applicants are looking for a job. They are on their absolute best behavior during the interview process. Applicants come in all scrubbed up, looking so fresh and pretty. Wide awake with plenty of coffee in the system. So attentive to your questions. So polite. In such a good mood.

Wow, they would make a great fit.

They have never met a sour customer. They have never had a situation overwhelm them. They can, according to their testimony, do it all perfectly.

Then comes the first week at work. They arrive for work with their hair a mess, unkempt clothes, and a sour mood. *Where is the person we interviewed,* you wonder?

Let's face it, hiring new team members is a bit of a subjective, inherently flawed process. You win some, and you lose some. We have all seen new team members come aboard. They interviewed well, but often they are not

Section 5: Build and Nurture a World-Class Team

the right fit. They certainly are not the person we thought they were when we hired them. The question posed by managers is, *How can I get better at identifying who will be a good fit? What process are we missing?*

We have asked these questions at Oak Haven for years. We have realized that hiring and onboarding a new team member requires buy-in from the entire team. So, in recent years, we have involved more team members in the interview and selection process. Our thinking is, if more team members are involved in the selection process, they will have more of a sense of responsibility to make sure the new team member has a successful transition. When current team members have been part of the selection process, there is more of an obligation to make sure the new hire is successful. There is also less complaining about any deficiencies the new hire might have and more patience in the process of getting them up to speed.

Because of this, we allow the entire team to weigh in on the applicant before the final selection is made. They get a chance to watch the applicant in a working interview. They can speak with them and ask questions. We often will take a final applicant to lunch and invite team members to join us. This allows the team to see the applicant in a more casual setting. There is a higher chance the applicant will let down their guard and show us a little more accurately who they really are. However, even with these processes in place, we don't always make the right call.

As we have thought about our hiring process and tried to improve it, we have started to change our emphasis slightly. We have begun to worry less about selecting the right person from the interview process. We have spent more time and energy communicating who we are as a company. We have taken time to describe our vision, our mission, and our culture. We have attempted to communicate more clearly in our job descriptions and our website what we as a company stand for. We have also tried to describe more accurately what the ideal candidate looks like. From the very start of the interview process, applicants are given an Oak Haven Way card. This card helps us communicate many of our ideals and values. Our hope is that

Leadership: Building and Nurturing a World-Class Team of Massage Therapists

by communicating these concepts, the right people will find us. Our intent is to be more effective in bringing aboard the most compatible and talented team members possible.

Improving the Interview Process for the Front Desk

Below are some of the recent changes we have made, or are making, to improve the selection process.

- Use a skills assessment tool such as a typing test or Excel test.
- Have applicants write a short statement about how they can help "raise the bar" in the area of customer service.
- Have applicants write about which of our core values they most relate to and why.
- Give the applicant an email from an unhappy customer and ask them to write a brief letter in response.
- Encourage everyone on the team to be part of the hiring process. Invite all team members to come in for the final interview so they can all weigh in. Not all team members will want to come in if it's a day off, but at least they have a choice to be part of the decision to bring on a new team member.
- Take the applicant to lunch and see how their personality comes through in a non-interview setting.

Over time, can we gear the hiring process to weigh what a candidate *does* rather than what they *say*. It is easy to give the answers the interviewer wants to hear. I am convinced this is at the core of the "what did you do with the person I interviewed" phenomenon.

A Bias Toward "No"

In *Radical Candor*, Kim Scott says, "If you are not dying to hire somebody, don't make an offer. Even if you are dying to hire somebody, allow yourself

Section 5: Build and Nurture a World-Class Team

to be overruled by the other interviewers who feel strongly the person should not be hired. In general, a bias toward no is useful when hiring."

Leave a Positive Impression

What can we do to leave a positive impression with all job candidates, even those we don't hire? Examine the interview process, make sure to let the applicants know their status and inform applicants when the decision has been made.

All Applicants are Potential Customers

"Each applicant is not only a possible future customer, but as things change over time, they may very well be a successful candidate at some point in the future. I want to offer one word of caution about the candidate screening process. Successful candidates will generally be delighted to receive a job offer. But what about the people who aren't offered a job? In many cases, these people far outnumber the people who are hired. It's important to design a selection process that treats all candidates with dignity and respect. Companies frequently waste candidates' time with multiple steps that often don't really matter in the selection process. Some fail to notify rejected applicants of their status. Keep in mind that all job applicants are potential customers. They may choose whether or not to do business with your company in the future based on their experience with the selection process. They may encourage or discourage friends and family to apply for an open position based on their impression of your organizational culture. If it all possible, you want job applicants to love your organization, even if they don't get to join it. It's

Leadership: Building and Nurturing a World-Class Team of Massage Therapists

important to note that they may also develop into qualified applicants at some point in the future."

Hiring for Culture

According to David Friedman, you can make a couple of errors as part of bringing aboard an applicant who is ultimately not the right fit.

"The first mistake is a failure to recognize the signs or to read the applicant's signals properly. This is not unusual, and it's one we will never eliminate entirely. People aren't always easy to read. Sometimes we don't pick up on a sign, or we simply misjudged a person. An interview is a pretty artificial environment, and we don't always get to know the real person. They're on their best behavior, and they're naturally trying to show us what we want to see.

"The second mistake is meeting someone we know isn't a good cultural fit for the company, but we hire them anyway. This is the mistake we have to avoid, and it's totally within our control. Unfortunately, I see this mistake far more frequently than the first one.

"Why would we hire someone we know isn't a good fit? There are a variety of common reasons. Sometimes we convince ourselves that the person possesses a skill that's important enough to us that we're willing to overlook the rest of the picture. Other times, we think we're going to be able to change them. The most common reason, however, is pure desperation. We're short-staffed in a particular department, we've been looking for some time and haven't been able to find the right person. Sometimes we are simply tired of interviewing, and we want the process to stop, so we can get back to doing our "work." It's as if we're comparing them to an empty chair rather than comparing them to what we really need. So, we hire them and figure we will just deal with it later. Six months later, we have to fire the person and clean up the mess created by our

Section 5: Build and Nurture a World-Class Team

shortsightedness. And then, of course, we still must go through the hiring process again and do it right. But at the moment, it just felt more comfortable to hire them and put the process behind us.

"While it sounds so simple, it takes a tremendous amount of leadership and discipline to avoid this mistake. In the theoretical world, it's easy. But in the real world, we are faced with these pressures and challenges. We do need to fill positions to complete projects and serve our customers. Despite this, we need to maintain our discipline and refuse to bring in people we don't believe will be a good fit.

"Before we go further, I want to be clear about two important points.

"**First**, when I talk about the importance of only hiring people who will be an excellent cultural fit, I'm not at all suggesting that it's okay to hire people who don't have the talent, skills, knowledge, or experience that we are looking for. I am assuming you found that, but in addition, the person has to also be an excellent cultural fit. It's not one or the other; it's both.

"**Second**, saying that someone is or isn't a good fit has nothing to do with their gender, ethnicity, religion, or whether or not they are a good person. She may be a wonderful human being, and we could be great friends, but that doesn't make her a good fit in the culture we are trying to build. This is about fit, not about judging a person's worth as a human being."

There are a couple of items worth noting from David Friedman's quote above.

- Attempt to hire for both components of fit, the technical side and the cultural side. If you want to build a powerful, effective business, that happens to the degree you can attract a talented team.

Leadership: Building and Nurturing a World-Class Team of Massage Therapists

- A team is only as effective as the culture they are working in. As you bring in team members, pay very close attention to the cultural fit of each potential team member.
- Hire for cultural fit in addition to all of the specific skill sets you were looking for.
- If they are not the right cultural fit, don't hire them. It is much less painful to continue interviewing, even for several additional weeks, than bring aboard a bad cultural fit.

An Additional Note About Cultural Fit

It's not always possible to get the cultural fit right, just like you don't always get the skill set right. We make our decisions to hire based on the information we have at the time, as limited as that information might be. Once we bring the applicant aboard, it becomes obvious if you have made the right choice or not. If it turns out you missed something with the applicant or misjudged something, and the person is not a good fit, either in their skill set or the cultural area, you must move them out of the organization as fast as possible. Hence the saying "hire slow, fire fast." We will talk about the process of dismissing a team member later in this section.

If you have the digital version of this book, you can click on the link below to listen to an excellent podcast on the importance of hiring correctly with Patrick Lencioni.

https://podcasts.apple.com/us/podcast/at-the-table-with-patrick-lencioni/id1474171732?i=1000446318931

Section 5: Build and Nurture a World-Class Team

ATTRACT ⇒ HIRE ⇒ ONBOARD ⇒ DEVELOP ⇒ RETAIN

Onboarding Team Members

Onboarding is every bit as important as every other step. The manner in which onboarding happens, the care and attention to detail during the onboarding process, can make or break an incoming team member. We must devote time and energy to choreographing every aspect of the new team member's first two weeks. Onboarding is the area that most companies give the least amount of attention to, and it is one of the most important. So much time is spent on the hiring process and finding the perfect candidate, and almost no thought is given to how they will be integrated with the team.

Here are some things we are doing or are in the process of initiating as part of our onboarding effort. These processes will look different depending on the position of the new team member.

The First Week

According to David Friedman in *Culture by Design*, "The first week a new employee spends in your company is actually the most important week in their entire career. It's that impactful. As critical as the first week is, it's remarkable how few companies spend appropriate time and resources **orchestrating every aspect of a new hire's early experience**. Instead, we spend huge amounts of time and money on recruiting and then give scant attention to how the new person starts."

Integrating New Hires into Oak Haven's Culture

Remember, first impressions of the company and the onboarding process actually start long before the new team member's first day on the job. First

105

impressions begin with the initial phone call to schedule the interview. First impressions happen in the setting of the interview appointment and the time spent in the waiting area before the interview. It all matters.

How can we improve this process? How might the initial phone call send a powerful message to the applicant about who we are and the type of culture we have? How can we do a better and more impressive job at onboarding and orienting new team members? How can we make their first two weeks the most impactful time of their entire career with Oak Haven? How can we make a powerful first impression on a new team member? Perhaps dinner or lunch with managers and/or Steven, Kathleen, and Allison during the first week of service?

Maybe a presentation by Steven about the Oak Haven Way during the first week would help impact a new team member?

The Buddy Program

Several years ago, we implemented a buddy program to give the new member a point of contact. This also served as a way to start the process of integrating the new hire into the social side of the company. The buddy would introduce the new team member to other staff members. They would also invite them out to lunch or for a drink to kickstart the integration within the first week. The whole point is to somehow get the new team member into the social fabric of Oak Haven Massage as quickly as possible. Starting a new job is exciting for the new team member, but it's scary at the same time. They are asking themselves a lot of questions as they start their new position with us. Questions such as:

- Did I make the right decision in choosing this company?
- Will I fit in here?
- Will I be able to make friends here?
- Will I enjoy my work?
- Can I do the work well enough?

Section 5: Build and Nurture a World-Class Team

Hopefully, having a buddy to guide them through the process will make it easier to integrate into the Oak Haven culture.

Have Business Cards Ready

Before the initial start date, we could take time to order business cards for the new team member and have them ready for them on their start date.

A Book with All Employees

As of May 2, 2020, Oak Haven Massage has 210 team members. It would be helpful for a new team member to have a book with all employees' photos for use as a reference. It could be divided up into management, administration, front desk, and therapists.

Onboarding Welcome Box

The two weeks between a new employee accepting a job offer and starting the job are the most critical. We want new team members to feel a part of our team from the moment they accept our offer, not just once they actually start on day one. As part of this effort, we send out a box of items to welcome the new member to Oak Haven. This box includes books, a t-shirt, a water bottle, and assorted other goodies.

How can we tweak the onboarding process to reinforce company values and minimize any loss of employees due to a haphazard and unplanned onboarding process?

We are doing better than we have ever done, but let's think of how we can make the onboarding process a more impactful experience.

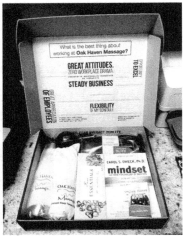

Initial Training for the Front Desk Team Member

Years ago, we would bring a new front desk team member aboard, and after an hour or two of orientation, start them immediately at the front desk dealing with real customers. This is similar to a swimming coach teaching his new students to swim by throwing them in the deep end of the pool. It was a bit of an intense experience for the new team member.

It took many years, but we finally realized we needed to start our new front desk team members with a week or two of intensive customer service and software training. This training-based approach to onboarding has caused less trauma and made the first two weeks on the job a better experience. New team members can learn in the safe environment of a simulated training session rather than directly in front of a waiting client.

Once we started this method of onboarding, we realized how important it was. We also realized how much pain we had been putting so many new workers through for so many years. To make the initial training better, we asked our newest team members a series of questions at the two-week mark:

- How could we make the initial training better?

Section 5: Build and Nurture a World-Class Team

- Where do you wish the training was more complete?
- What do you wish you had known earlier in the training process?

The First Day for Office Staff

This is usually a training day for front office staff. It would be good if the manager or other corporate leaders could go out to lunch on the first day with the new team member. This would serve as a way of welcoming them.

And as far as training goes, it would be excellent to give them a book for the upcoming training with the entire sequence of training outlined.

The First Day for Massage Therapists

This will be a day for orientation. New therapists will be shown where to find supplies such as linens and massage lotion. We will introduce the new therapists to the client intake process and information on setting up the massage room. We will also go over the end of session protocols. The new therapist will view several hours of video to prepare for their first actual client. Their first day could involve working on only staff to ease into the process. Here, too, it might be nice to schedule a lunch with the manager and/or other leaders as a way of welcoming them and showing support. They are wondering if they have made the correct choice in joining our company. Let's show them they have.

Massage therapists will also receive their business cards on their first day and be sent a welcome box with assorted items.

Leadership: Building and Nurturing a World-Class Team of Massage Therapists

ATTRACT ➡ HIRE ➡ ONBOARD ➡ DEVELOP ➡ RETAIN

Develop Team Members

Do you remember our definition of a leader? A leader is "anyone who takes responsibility for finding the potential in people and processes and has the courage to **develop** that potential."

In this section, we will discuss the role of leadership in developing a team. The desire and ability to develop people will separate a mediocre manager from a genuinely great manager. There are several components for greatness in the area of developing your team.

Philosophy

It all starts with your internal philosophy, your belief. Allow me to explain. The manager must believe that people can develop and become more effective over time. It's vital that managers have the belief that people can learn, with effort, to serve the needs of the customer at a higher level. (This philosophical position is at the core of the book *Mindset*, which is summarized in Appendix 2.)

Desire

Great managers want to impact people. It's in their DNA. They almost can't help themselves.

Effective managers want to see people grow. This often comes from their own experience with growth and development. Gaining an understanding of how powerful it can be to experience personal growth is often at the heart of wanting it for others.

Method/Curriculum

You will need to have a plan for developing people. What do you want them to learn? How will you teach them? It can take years to create a series of lessons and training for your team. The development of training and its improvement is an ongoing, never-ending process. We will not get into the specifics of training development in this book. We have two books that cover the training process reasonably well.

We have *Creating a World-Class Customer Experience* for the front desk staff, and *Massage and Bodywork – Practice Essentials* for the massage therapists. These two books form the foundation of our training at Oak Haven Massage.

Time/Money

It takes time and money to train and develop people. It is an investment in the future of the company. You must look at your business philosophy; how important is it for you from a philosophical perspective to develop people? Do you have the "stomach" for spending time, energy, and money on training and developing people?

Leadership: Building and Nurturing a World-Class Team of Massage Therapists

Some will say, "What if we train them and they leave?" A better question might be, "What if you don't train them, and they stay?"

Commitment

It's the time and the money involved in training that will test your commitment level. How important is developing people to your overall philosophy of business? If it's imperative, the training will likely continue and develop over time. If it's not really that important, the time and money spent will cause training and development to eventually fade away.

Five Critical Practices for Growing Your Team

Managers are less bosses and more **mentors**, **examples**, and **coaches**. Their goal is to bring out the best in the team members they lead. Below are five practices that will help you develop and mentor your team.

1. Career Conversations
2. Set Expectations
3. Train
4. Seek feedback
5. Give feedback

1. Career Conversations

One of the essential functions of a manager is to mentor team members. Effective mentoring requires you first know the person you are trying to help. Every person on your team has different backgrounds, interests, and goals. Before you give direction, seek to know the team member's personal history and career goals. Understand people's motivations and ambitions to help them take a step in the direction of their dreams.

Kim Scott, in her excellent book *Radical Candor*, spoke of three conversations managers should have with their team members.

Section 5: Build and Nurture a World-Class Team

Conversation One: Life story

Scott suggested a simple opening to these conversations. "Starting with kindergarten, tell me about your life." Then focus on the choices people have made and try to understand why they have made those choices. The purpose of this conversation is to get to know the team member at a deeper level.

Conversation Two: Dreams

The second conversation moves from understanding what motivates people to understanding the person's dreams. Find out what they want to achieve at the apex of their career. What vision do they have for their life? Scott chose the word "dreams" very consciously. Bosses usually ask about "long-term goals" or "career aspirations" or "five-year plans," but each of these phrases, when used by a boss, tends to elicit a certain type of answer: a professional, and not entirely human, answer. It also invites a response that the person imagines the boss wants to hear rather than a description of what the person really wants to achieve.

Conversation Three: Eighteen-month Plan

Last, get people to begin asking themselves the following questions:

- What do I need to learn to move in the direction of my dreams?
- How should I prioritize the things I need to learn?
- Whom can I learn from?
- How can I change my role to learn it?

An excellent book to expound on this topic is Matthew Kelly's *The Dream Manager*. I Highly recommend it.

113

Leadership: Building and Nurturing a World-Class Team of Massage Therapists

2. Set Expectations

Let your team members know what is expected of them. Tell your employees your business vision and goals, how their job fits in, and how they can actively participate in making the workplace successful. A purpose-driven employee is a powerful force in any organization.

3. Train

Training is one of the **five critical practices for growing your team**. I wanted to include it here for the sake of completeness, but training is such a huge part of Oak Haven Massage, I will not attempt to cover it here. Just know that we train from the moment a new team member sets foot inside the door until the day they leave. It is ingrained in our culture. The first behavior on the Oak Haven Way card is, "Be a lifelong learner. Seek to learn and develop as a person, as a professional, and as a team member. A growth mindset matters."

Training people is a crucial function of growing the team.

4. Seek Feedback

Here are some questions to regularly ask your team members. These questions can be asked any time, but they might be suitable for your one on one.

- What aspects of your job do you think are a good fit for you?
- Are there parts of your job that you believe you're not very good at?
- What can I do to help you do your best work?
- Is there any feedback you have for me regarding my leadership and management style?
- How would you describe the culture of our team and organization? What parts of the culture do you like the most? Where could it be better?

Section 5: Build and Nurture a World-Class Team

- What's your career vision? What does your ideal next job in the company look like?
- Is there anything that our team should be focused on that we're not already?
- Are there any projects that you'd like to work on that you currently are not?
- Can you share what your top work goals are for the next few months? How can I help you achieve them?

5. Give Feedback

In *Radical Candor*, Kim Scott says this of feedback:

"Employees want and need regular feedback, and the lack of it is one of the biggest reasons people find other jobs. Often, employees only hear from their bosses when they make a mistake.

"When an employee does something that shows talent, initiative, problem-solving, or success with a project or task, let him know. When you recognize and reinforce performance or behaviors, employees tend to repeat them.

"It is also vital for managers to promptly confront problems and provide the team members honest but respectful coaching. Even your best employees want to know how they can do better; this is how they became your top people. If you see a performance opportunity or a performance gap, work with the employee to develop an action plan. One small change can have a positive impact on an employee's overall performance. Formally, and at least once a year, employees want you to review their performance. This is your opportunity to discuss an employee's accomplishments, opportunities for growth and improvement, and professional career development. If he had some challenges during the year, you can review the progress he made. And remember: Don't save

Leadership: Building and Nurturing a World-Class Team of Massage Therapists

performance and behavior problems until the annual review meeting. Deal with them along the way so issues don't build up."

How to Help Team Members Who Want to Contribute More

Every organization has people in it who want to have a greater impact. Sometimes we lose great team members because they didn't see a way to advance in the company. Teach team members to look for opportunities that exist around them. Teach them to look for needs in their own niche within the company. Team members who interact with customers and other coworkers every day are in a perfect position to see what is and is not working in their particular part of the business. They are in the best position to see needs that should be filled. They are in the best place to notice a chance to make Oak Haven better. Managers can teach team members to keep their eyes open and watch for opportunities. When they see needs, gaps, processes, or positions that should be in place but are not, teach them to bring these ideas forward. Let me give you a couple of examples of team members who have observed a need, outlined a solution, and then submitted a proposal to fill the needs they observed.

Ivan, one of our instructors in Austin saw the need for personal, one-on-one instruction and mentoring. He came to the manager with a proposal to do a personalized mentoring session for therapists who needed it. Management gave him the green light. He now does personal mentoring in both Austin and San Antonio.

Jessica, a long-time front desk team member, saw that we were trying to develop a more cohesive workplace culture. She came across *The Five Languages of Appreciation in the Workplace*. She also thought of several areas where we could enhance our employee recognition. She asked for a meeting with the management staff. She gave a presentation on how we could raise the level of employee recognition using the languages of appreciation. She also had ideas for other ways to engage in employee recognition. The

116

Section 5: Build and Nurture a World-Class Team

managers loved the idea and created a 20-hour a week position for her. She started the position of employee recognition coordinator. Jessica has been in the role for the past several years.

Jill joined Oak Haven Massage several years ago and became very involved in the training classes. She noticed over the years, as the classes started to increase, a class coordinator was needed. She proposed a position where someone would work to promote the courses and help people sign up. This person would also remind the students of the classes the day before and keep a log of classes attended by each student. She put together an outline of what a class coordinator would do. And, you guessed it, she was given the position. She now coordinates classes in both Austin and San Antonio. She saw a need, recommended a solution and created a position.

Lindsey, manager in San Antonio, came to Allison and I to recommend we open an additional location in San Antonio. We thought about it and agreed. Lindsey is now the regional director in the San Antonio area. She has three locations under her direction. She saw a need, and recommended a course of action.

Hopefully, you have seen a pattern with these stories. People saw a need, came up with a plan, proposed the plan, and sometimes created a new position. Proposals do not always have such a positive ending, but if you never try, it never happens.

Three Intersecting Circles

For those team members who want to contribute more but are not sure what they might propose, teach them about the three circles.

Think of three circles, each representing:

1. What you enjoy doing.
2. Your skill set.
3. Your skills value to the organization.

Then, look at where they intersect:

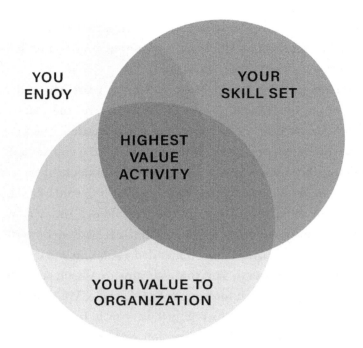

Where these three circles intersect is possibly something that would benefit the organization. It's often in the best interest of the business to have team members doing what they are good at and enjoy doing. Provided these areas are also valuable to the company. Teach team members to look for when these three circles intersect. It could be a win-win solution for both the team member and the organization.

Leaders Develop Other Leaders

Leaders shouldn't worry about holding on to their turf. We do see the leader occasionally who hesitates to develop other leaders. Perhaps these leaders feel threatened or think that by holding others back, their position is more secure. The wise leader does not think this way. The confident

Section 5: Build and Nurture a World-Class Team

leader knows the only way they can advance is by training and developing those under their direction.

Leadership Pivots

It is interesting to note that, as you are working your way into a leadership position, it's often all about you. You getting noticed, you getting credit, you getting praise. When you become a leader, everything changes. We say a pivot occurs. Now your task as a leader is to take the focus off you and shine the light on your team. Now, the team gets noticed, the team gets the credit, the team gets the praise. You turn into the team's advocate, allowing your team to shine and be recognized. This ability to pivot and shine the light on your team is a separate skill set, and it's certainly a different mindset.

Here are some examples of ways that thinking changes, or should change, once you become a leader.

FROM	TO
Always knowing	Always learning
Knowing	Curious
I	We (When Discussing Wins)
We	I (When discussing problems)
Criticizing	Recommend solutions
Finding problems	Catching team members doing stuff right
Seeking acknowledgement/ praise	Giving acknowledgement/praise
Seeking the credit	Giving the credit to the team
Looking out for yourself	Looking out for the team & business

119

Leadership: Building and Nurturing a World-Class Team of Massage Therapists

Rock Stars and Superstars

Unfortunately, for too long, I believed that pushing everybody to grow super-fast was simply "best practice" for building a high-performing team. I was always looking for the best, the brightest, the brashest, and the most ambitious. For the first twenty years of my career, it never occurred to me that some people did not want the next, bigger job.

Then a leader at Apple pointed out to me that all teams need stability as well as growth to function properly; nothing works well if everyone is gunning for the next promotion. She called the people on her team who got exceptional results but who were on a more gradual growth trajectory "**rock stars**" because they were like the Rock of Gibraltar on her team (not because they liked rock and roll). These people loved their work and were world-class at it, but they didn't want her job or to be Steve Jobs. They were happy where they were. The people who were on a steeper growth trajectory—the ones who'd go crazy if they were still doing the same job in a year—she called "**superstars**." They were the source of growth on any team. She was adamant about needing a balance of both.

The rock stars love their work. They have found their groove. They do not want the next job if it takes them away from their craft. Not all artists want to own a gallery; in fact, most do not. If you honor and reward the rock stars, they will become the people you most rely on. If you promote them into roles they do not want or aren't suited for, you often will lose them—or, even worse, wind up firing them. Superstars, on the other hand, need to be challenged and given new opportunities to grow continuously.

The most important thing you can do for your team collectively is to understand what growth trajectory each person wants to be on at a given time and whether that matches the team's needs and

Section 5: Build and Nurture a World-Class Team

opportunities. Reward your rock stars. Don't give all the glory to the superstars.

Super Stars

Here's some advice about what to do when you are lucky enough to have superstars on your team. The best way to keep superstars happy is to challenge them and make sure they are continually learning. It's vital not to "squash" these people. Recognize that you'll probably be working for them one day and celebrate that fact.

Understanding What Matters and Why

To be successful at growth management, you need to find out what motivates each person on your team. You also need to learn what each person's long-term ambitions are and understand how their current circumstances fit their motivations and life goals. Get to know your direct reports well enough to know why they care about their work. Learn what they hope to get out of their careers. Once you understand this, you can put the right people in the right roles and assign the right projects to the right people.

"Steep growth" is generally characterized by rapid change— learning new skills or deepening existing ones quickly. It's not about becoming a manager—plenty of individual contributors remain on a steep growth trajectory their entire careers, and plenty of managers are on a gradual growth trajectory. It's about having an increased impact over time. Gradual growth is characterized by stability. People on a gradual growth trajectory, who perform well, have generally mastered their work, and are making incremental rather than sudden, dramatic improvements. Some roles may be better suited to a rock star because they require steadiness,

121

accumulated knowledge, and attention to detail. Someone in a superstar phase might not have the focus or patience for a slower pace.

Generally, people in a superstar phase are bad at rock star roles, and people in a rock star phase will hate a superstar role.

Managing Rock Stars

What's the best way to manage rock stars, the people whom you can count on to deliver great results year after year? You need to recognize them to keep them happy. For too many bosses, "recognition" means "promotion." But in most cases, this is a big mistake. Promotion often puts these people in roles they are not as well-suited for or don't want. The key is to recognize their contribution in other ways. It may be a bonus or a raise. Or, if they like public speaking, get them to present at your all-hands meetings or other big events. If they like teaching, get them to help new people learn their roles faster. Or if they are shy, make sure that you and others on the team thank them privately for the work they do. Consider, carefully, tenure awards. If your organization gives performance ratings and/or bonuses, make sure they are fair to the rock stars.

Not Every Superstar Wants to Manage

Lack of interest in managing is not the same thing as being on a gradual growth trajectory. At the same time, interest in managing is not the same as being on a steep growth trajectory. **Management and growth should not be equated.**

Google's engineering teams solved this problem by creating an "individual contributor" career path that is more prestigious than the manager path and sidesteps management entirely. When

Section 5: Build and Nurture a World-Class Team

management is the only path to higher compensation, the quality of management suffers, and the lives of the people who work for these reluctant managers become miserable.

Promotions

Be fair. Few things can create a sense of injustice on a team like having a boss who promotes based on favoritism, or a manager who promotes people much faster than the manager sitting in the next office. Another version of the bad promotion occurs when people are competent for the next job but have no desire to do it at that moment in their lives. I once had a colleague who'd planned carefully so that when he had his first baby, he was in a job that he'd mastered and thus could get home to be with his newborn. His boss, however, had different plans for him: a promotion. When informed of his promotion, the man declined it. When told it wasn't optional, he quit. What a waste. Don't do this to your rock stars! Part of building a cohesive team is to create a culture that recognizes and rewards the rock stars. I'm afraid for most of my career I treated them like second-class citizens. I'm grateful that my experiences at Apple set me straight.

Avoid Promotion/Status Obsession

I once became totally paralyzed over my keyboard when trying to write the email I was supposed to send out to my whole team at Google to celebrate promotions. Ten years later, I finally understand what was wrong: I shouldn't have been writing that email at all. Announcing promotions breeds unhealthy competition for the wrong things: documentation of status rather than development of skill. If a promotion includes a change of role, then announce it. But not every change of role signifies a promotion.

123

Gurus

Another great way to highlight how great people are at a job is to acknowledge them as gurus in their area of expertise. You might recognize their mastery by putting the person in charge of teaching others the skill. Give them a couple of months to develop a class.

Retain

Retention could be thought of as the end result if you have done the preceding four steps correctly. Retention is what happens when you:

- Attract and hire the right people in the first place.
- Bring aboard people who are inspired by the company's vision and mission.
- Identify people who want to serve the customer at a high level.
- Recruit team members who want to be part of a well-oiled team.
- Properly onboard new team members.
- Engage in a constant effort to get to know your people on a personal level.
- Assist team members in personal and professional growth and development.

Retention also happens when you make the distinction between rock stars and superstars. It's critical to help each group to get what they want and need.

Retention will increase when you move out those who are not the right fit for the team. The process of moving out the wrong people serves to

Section 5: Build and Nurture a World-Class Team

decrease workplace conflict, strife, gossip, and overall tension, creating a happier place to work.

The following items are a few areas that factor into the retention equation. Some of these items have or will be mentioned in other places in this book. I include some of these items here as well for emphasis and completeness. There are many components to creating a business that people want to be a part of. Of course, the reasons are as varied as there are people. We are all motivated and influenced in different ways and for various reasons. We are all in different circumstances in our lives, and have different needs and wants. Some will place a high priority on salary. Others will look more at flexibility of schedule. Some will stay or leave based on advancement opportunities. Others will look at the presence or absence of friends in the workplace. But generally, the items listed below are many of the areas that team members will be evaluating when deciding to stay or leave a company. Many of the items below factor into retention to some degree.

Culture

It has a profound impact on many aspects of the business. It plays a big part in team members choosing to stay with the company. Culture could be thought of as a composite of many of the items listed below.

A Feeling of Belonging/Team Spirit/Friends

This area might be thought of as the social side of the workplace. Humans are social creatures and naturally want to be part of a group. Team members will be motivated to stay or leave based on the degree they feel part of the group and have friends at work.

Work Conditions

By work conditions, I am referring to how people are generally treated by management. Do the team members feel valued? Or do they feel expendable? Are they treated with respect or disdain? Does the boss have a win-win attitude, or does the supervisor need to win every time? Do team members feel a sense of gratitude from those who manage? Are communications to team members respectful, polite, and courteous?

Opportunity for advancement

The presence or absence of advancement opportunities are a factor in some decisions to stay or leave the company. The nature of the business and the level of growth in the industry play a part in this. Not all companies have abundant opportunities for advancement.

Compensation

Annual salary and benefits are an important consideration for a team member's decision to stay or leave. This is highly variable from person to person. Not everyone looks at work from any single vantage point, such as salary. Not everyone is motivated in the same way by money. It is an error management often makes to assume others are inspired by the same things that motivate the manager. Oak Haven's philosophy is to have salaries at the top of the industry range. But we realize there are often other more important considerations.

Recognition

For some, recognition factors into the decision to stay or leave a company. . Recognition simply means don't take people for granted.

Recognition can take many forms:

- A thank you note from a manager.
- A bonus for a job well done.
- A shoutout for advancement or for a work anniversary.
- A birthday card.

There are a lot of ways to recognize and show appreciation. It's interesting to note that we all have preferred ways to be shown appreciation. We have a

Section 5: Build and Nurture a World-Class Team

segment we teach in the leadership training based on *The Five Languages of Appreciation in the Workplace* by Gary Chapman. It's a wonderful reminder that we all have preferred ways to be shown we are appreciated.

Appreciation

It's important to show appreciation to our team. If a team member feels valued and appreciated by management, it factors a lot into longevity.

Below is a summary of four of the languages of appreciation from Gary Chapman's book *The Five Languages of Appreciation in the Workplace*.

The book's central theme is that it's important to show appreciation in the "language" of the recipient, not in the "language" or way you would want to be shown appreciation. We all have preferred ways to be shown appreciation. The fifth language, physical touch, has been left off for obvious reasons.

1. **Words of Affirmation**

   Some team members will prefer verbal affirmations of how much they are appreciated. This language uses words to communicate a positive message to another person. When you speak this language, you are verbally affirming a positive characteristic about a person.

2. **Quality Time**

   Some team members feel valued when you spend time with them. You may need to clarify how your coworker prefers to spend quality time. It might be in a small group outing, one-on-one lunch, during a lunch break at work, after work, or a volunteer event.

3. **Acts of Service**

   For some people, receiving a gesture or act of service speaks to them. A person who has acts of service as their primary language feels appreciated and cared for when others reach out to help them. For them, actions speak louder than words.

127

4. **Tangible Gifts**

For other team members, giving them a small gift is the best way to show your appreciation. When we talk about giving gifts in the workplace, it is important to understand that we are speaking of small items that show you are thinking about them. A breakfast taco will often work beautifully.

Connection with the Vision-Mission of the Company

It should come as no surprise that people will often base decisions to stay with a company due to their connection to the company's mission and vision. If you doubt this, just look at the numbers of volunteers that stay with churches, food banks, and other worthwhile nonprofit organizations. They often stay for years without a salary at all. They stay because they believe in what the organization stands for. They feel connected to its mission, and they have a sense of making a difference. For some, this is their highest priority.

Growth

For some team members, personal and professional growth is their greatest need. They look for a company where they feel they can reach their potential. The decision is easy for these team members; if they are growing and developing, they will stay. When they stop growing, they will look for other opportunities.

Willingness to Accommodate Schedules

With some team members, the single most crucial aspect of their work is their schedule. A small item, but for some, this is an important factor in their decision to stay with the company.

Burnout

Burnout is a real issue for many team members. This issue seems to be particularly significant with our customer-facing front office staff. Dealing

Section 5: Build and Nurture a World-Class Team

with customer issues all day, every day can be taxing and can lead to burn-out. We are sensitive to this reality and have made several considerations to help minimize burnout among front desk team members.

These include:

- Shorter schedules
- Higher pay
- More vacation time
- Added attention to building camaraderie among the staff

The Manager

It is said, "people join companies, but they quit managers." A manager might be the most significant single factor on this list. One reason managers are so important in retaining team members is that they not only influence so many of the other factors listed above, they are all under the manager's direct control.

Being successful at retention does not mean you keep team members for-ever. Oak Haven has a limited number of ways to move up the ladder. Some team members would like to develop into management. Unfortunately, we may not always have a management place for them. Massage therapy is a very physical profession. As therapists grow older and their bodies change, they may look for other jobs that are not as physically difficult. There can be many reasons why someone may want to eventually move on from Oak Haven. When they do, we send them off with our love and support, wish-ing them all the success in their new venture.

Thoughts on the Firing Process

It might seem slightly ironic to find us talking about firing, after all our efforts to attract, hire, onboard, develop, and retain. But the truth is, moving people out who are not right for the team is a critical piece of the formula for building powerful teams. Sometimes the best thing you can do to lift the group is to remove a non-compatible member.

129

According to David Salyers, author and VP of Chick-fil-a, in his book *Remarkable*, there are three types of people who will **rapidly disrupt an organization's culture**.

1. **Victims** – These people view problems as personal persecutions rather than challenges to overcome.
2. **Nay-sayers** – People who are perpetually pessimistic and fulfill their own negative prophecies
3. **Know it all's** – These people are smarter than everyone else, at least in their mind. The main problem here is a lack of humility.

I couldn't agree more. Let's move these folks on to bigger and better opportunities.

In addition to the three groups above who should be moved out, there is a very useful way to evaluate if a team member is a right fit for the company. We call it the Performance/Culture Grid.

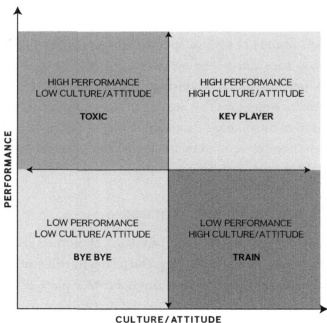

Section 5: Build and Nurture a World-Class Team

The Performance/Cultural Grid is a good aid in considering the dual aspects of a team member's performance and cultural fit.

When you consider the performance of a team member, they can be on a continuum from low to high on the performance axis. On the cultural axis, you rank their cultural fit, also on a continuum from low to high. If their performance is high and the cultural fit is high, they fall into the upper right quadrant—they are a **key player**. Take good care of these folks; they are your top people.

However, suppose someone is a top performer and falls very low on the cultural fit axis. In that case, these team members fall into the **toxic** quadrant. They remain with the company because of their high performance. Still, they often sew discord and negatively disrupt the culture. Dismissing these people is very difficult due to their high performance. It's not easy to dismiss a high performer. These people test your resolve to have a robust culture. We, as managers, usually keep these folks around way too long. They eventually find their way out of the company as managers become exasperated, but not before significant damage has occurred. A good manager will make the tough call and move these employees out sooner rather than later.

Let's discuss the people who are **low performers**. They also come in two varieties; one group of low performers are high on the cultural fit axis. They are in the bottom right quadrant. These are people we love, a perfect cultural fit. But they are not as good at their job as we would like. These are the people we want to **train**. These are the folks we want to work with and see if we can get them up to speed. The challenge for managers here is to decide when to keep moving forward with training, hoping for better performance. With these team members, we often spend precious time, energy, and money in training, and we never get the performance we need. It's difficult to know when to pull the plug and admit they may not be able to raise their performance levels. These people also test the manager's resolve, but in a different way. These folks will test how committed you are to build a world-class team. You send a powerful message to your team when you keep low performers just because they are nice people.

131

Leadership: Building and Nurturing a World-Class Team of Massage Therapists

Then you have another group of low performers. These people are low performing **and** they are not a good cultural fit. These are the people you move out as soon as it becomes apparent they are not a good fit. The sooner, the better.

General Guidelines for Firing

1. Firing is a process; it's not an event.
2. Most managers wait too long to dismiss non-performing, poor cultural fit team members. Better to do it sooner than wait too long. Do it as soon as you know it's not going to work out.
3. Don't make the decision unilaterally. Involve others who are impacted by the poor performing team member.

Giving Feedback

The firing process starts with making a valiant attempt at letting the team member know what behavior is needed and where they need improvement. We call this feedback.

Giving team members accurate, timely feedback is the first and most crucial step in avoiding dismissal. Don't forget that every team member we bring aboard was selected after weeks of interviews. We chose them out of several hundred applicants. We have spent weeks training these team members. We have a lot invested in them up to this point. We want it to work. But we need to be honest with them and let them know what we need from them.

Overview of the Feedback Process

The **first step** in feedback is often addressing concerns in a group setting. This serves as a way of educating the people involved. The thinking here is to assume they are not performing in ways we require because they have not been adequately trained or informed. So, we approach it with a non-threatening group discussion. In this discussion, we are not pointing any fingers at anyone. We are not calling anyone out specifically. When I say group, it

132

Section 5: Build and Nurture a World-Class Team

might be just a group of two people. You are just trying to avoid singling out someone by having a meeting with only them.

The potential challenge with this low-key approach is that the person who needs the direction will sometimes think you were talking to someone else and not them. So, they miss the point. If this low-key method does not accomplish your objective, you can always move on to step two. **Step two** is to meet with the person privately and review the issue in a very cordial way. Ask him/her politely for their help in this area and move on. Nothing heavy or serious. You are shooting for a very non-threatening discussion in the spirit of making them aware.

The third step in this process gets a bit more serious. And a bit more confrontational. If the first two attempts do not accomplish your objective, then schedule another meeting to outline the behavior you need to be changed. Make sure the team member knows this issue has the potential to affect their employment status. Let them know this problem is something they must deal with, or they may be released from the company. This third discussion may or may not include a formal write up.

As with all things managerial, this process is an art form. It could go a couple of different ways from here, depending on a wide variety of factors. If problems persist after this third meeting, you have a couple of choices for the fourth meeting.

The fourth meeting may very well be a dismissal. Dismissal, of course, is a serious consideration. Factors to consider may include:

- The nature of the issues you are dealing with.
- The attitude and disposition of the team member.
- The positive aspects they bring to the team and their job.

The fourth meeting may also be a final warning. This would serve to put the person on notice that we have reached the end of our willingness to continue dealing with this issue.

To Be or Not To Be Nitpicky

This brings up an interesting philosophical question. How much of a picky person should we be? How often should we bring things to our teams' attention? Should we be tolerant and overlook small stuff? Should we bring up everything?

These questions are difficult for managers. I would say that managers typically error on the side of not bringing issues up to team members. They don't want to seem nitpicky. This has the effect of allowing things to build up. When things are finally mentioned, it's often with a higher level of pent-up frustration and possibly even anger. It's far better to let people know of issues along the way. Don't let issues build up. Air on the side of nitpicky.

When It's Time to Fire

In many ways, *your job as the boss is to set and uphold a quality bar*. Holding to a standard can feel harsh in the short term. But, in the long term, the only thing that is meaner is lowering the bar. Don't get sucked into just avoiding or ignoring the problems when managing people who are doing okay but not great! Everybody can excel somewhere. And to build a great team that achieves exceptional results, everybody needs to be doing great work. Accepting mediocrity isn't good for anybody.

How do you know when it's time to fire somebody?

Have you given straightforward, honest guidance and feedback? Have you demonstrated to the team member that you care personally about their work and their life? Have you been crystal clear when you have challenged them to improve? Has your praise been substantive and specific about what they have done right, rather than simply a salve to their ego? Have you been humble as well as direct in your criticism, offering to help them find solutions rather than attacking them as a person? And have you done these things on multiple occasions over the course of time? If the answer is yes and you have not

Section 5: Build and Nurture a World-Class Team

seen improvement or have seen only flickers of progress, it's time. Remember, the definition of insanity is continuing to do the same thing and expecting different results. How is this person's poor performance affecting the rest of the team? As a manager, it's your job to make sure you understand everyone else's perspective, and how her poor performance affects other members of the team. Generally, by the time one of your direct report's poor performance has come to your attention, it's been driving their peers nuts for a long time. Have you sought out a second opinion, spoken to someone whom you trust and with whom you can talk the problem through? Sometimes you may think you've been clear when you haven't been. Getting an outside perspective can help you make sure you're being fair. Also, if you don't have experience firing somebody, talk to somebody who does.

Common lies managers tell themselves

Managers almost always wait too long to fire people. Being overly cautious may be preferable to being too hasty. Still, I'd say that most managers wait far too long to do it because they have fooled themselves into believing that it's unnecessary.

Below are three common lies managers tell themselves to avoid firing somebody:

1. **It will get better**

   But of course, it won't get better all by itself. So stop and ask yourself: how, exactly, will it get better? What are you going to do differently? What will the person in question do differently? How might circumstances change? Even if things have gotten a little better, have they improved enough? If you don't have a clear and concise answer to those questions, it probably won't get better.

2. **Somebody is better than nobody**

   Another common reason why bosses are reluctant to fire a poor performer is that they don't want a "hole" on the team. If you

135

fire Jeffrey, who will do the work he was doing? How long will it take you to find a replacement? The fact is that poor performers often create extra work for others. They leave parts of their job undone or do other parts sloppily. They behave unprofessionally in ways that others must compensate for. Steve Jobs put it succinctly, if harshly, when he said, "It's better to have a hole than an asshole."

3. **It's bad for morale**

Keeping someone who can't do the job is far worse for morale than firing them. Again, this comes down to having built a good relationship with the person you're firing. It comes back to having rapport. When you fire someone, you create the possibility for the person to excel and find happiness performing meaningful work elsewhere. Part of getting a good job is leaving a bad job, or one that's bad for you. Remember, it's not the person who sucks; it's the job that sucks—at least for this person. Retaining people who are doing bad work penalizes the people doing excellent work.

When the Decision Has Been Made

There will be times when all your efforts to help the person become a productive member of the team are unsuccessful. At some point, hopefully, sooner than later, you will decide you must dismiss the employee. This is never an easy decision. You realize it will have a significant impact on them and their family. But it must be done. You have done everything you could to prevent the dismissal. When the decision for dismissal is finally made, it's time for you to shift out of coaching mode and simply inform the team member of your decision.

If you have done all you could do up to this point, the person is likely expecting your meeting. They have very likely braced themselves for the inevitable. They know what the issues are, and they know they have not met your requirements.

136

Section 5: Build and Nurture a World-Class Team

You might say something like, "We've given it a fair shot, and it just isn't working out. I'm sorry, but I will have to let you go."

Depending on the circumstances, you could attempt to soften the blow by saying something like, "I just don't think this situation is a good fit for you," or, "I think it's time we allow you to just move on."

Here is a list of things you **should not** do when you let someone go:

- Get defensive.
- Explain why you have come to this decision.
- Make them wrong, or the fall guy.
- Try to justify your position.
- Get angry or demonstrate frustration.
- Try to coach the person on how they can learn from this for the future.

If you have done things correctly up to this point, you have already attempted to coach them. The time for coaching is over.

How Might a Team Member React

The reaction of a team member to being fired can be all over the spectrum of possibilities. Some will just quietly pack up their things and leave. Some will start crying. Some will get mad and start shouting. We have even had some people do physical damage to the building. Some will try to confront you. Some will give you a hug. It can be just about any reaction you could imagine. Each time it will be different.

Sometimes the person will press for reasons. "What could I have done differently?" Resist the urge to go into coaching. Just stick with, "It just is not a good fit," or, "I'm sorry it didn't work out." It is a trap, don't fall for it and stick to your script.

Some Dismissals are Different

Some dismissals are for gross negligence or gross misconduct. They may have been stealing, or they may have committed an act of abuse towards a client. For these cases of gross misconduct, we will not cut the person any slack. We will be as forceful as we need to be, including telling the person they will be reported to the police or the regulating agency.

Leave Employees with Dignity Intact

For others, who it really was just the wrong fit, we might give them a chance to resign instead of being fired. This has implications with unemployment, but it allows them to list on their resume that they terminated the relationship.

If possible, we want to send former team members back into the open labor market with their dignity and self-esteem intact. We are not looking to be right in our decision, and we have no interest in making them wrong or deficient. We want to be sensitive to the human emotions they may be feeling. They may be feeling a sense of loss. They are leaving friendships they care about. There may be a sense of embarrassment, feeling of failure, shame, regret, not to mention the loss of income and threat to their livelihood. These are heavy, significant emotions we wish to be sensitive to.

They are also dealing with a component of fear. They may be wondering how they will be able to provide for themselves and their family going forward. They are also very likely wondering how they will explain this to family members. When delivering the news, be clear, be brief, be kind, and be respectful. It is possible that in some situations, we might be able to provide severance pay. We might also ask how they would like us to explain their departure to coworkers. If it's possible to accommodate these requests, we will make every attempt to do so.

In summary: if a graceful exit is possible, it is preferable.

SECTION 6

Managing Conflict in the Workplace

THIS IS NOT MEANT TO BE THE DEFINITIVE WORD ON WORKPLACE conflict. This section is meant to be a starting place for discussion and to give us a common language. Many factors need to be considered as you develop the skills and techniques for tackling conflict in the workplace. We invite you to study this material to better understand some of the issues involved in workplace conflict.

Why Managing Conflict in the Workplace Matters

The topic of workplace conflict, in my opinion, comes under the general heading of, "What kind of workplace do we want? What do we want our culture to be like?"

It's not that we want our workplace to be conflict free; we want and encourage a degree of "healthy conflict." More on that important topic later.

This issue of managing conflict is essential for several reasons. It is challenging to raise the customer service bar if team members are dealing with strife and discord. Our impact on our customers is a team effort. Conflict thwarts teamwork by increasing discord, animosity, bitterness, and ill will. My interest in establishing Oak Haven Massage was to create a high

139

performing team. High-performing teams are more fun. High performing teams are more challenging to develop and maintain. Conflict and discord among team members reduce the effectiveness of the group. Strife and friction can create a challenging environment in which to spend our days.

At Oak Haven, this is how we choose to "play the game." Team members can come aboard and be part of a high-performance team or decide to join other groups where the expectations and standards are different.

Conflict and discord in the workplace can make it very difficult to attract and retain high performing individuals. Prospective team members may sense strife during the interview process and choose not to come aboard. A new team member might join the business but quickly realize they have made a mistake and leave the company. When conflict and discord take center stage in a company, it will drive away those who are not prone to drama and disharmony. If managers don't remove the agitators, the group will have only the cranky, cantankerous, unhappy folks remaining. I am willing to concede that it takes intention, design thought, and effort to build a divergent group into a high performing team, but I think it's worth it.

Let's try to understand what lies at the heart of conflict in the workplace. Let's look at how we can minimize conflict between co-workers. I say minimize because, as long as we are dealing with humans, we will never be able to fully eradicate conflict.

Exploring Workplace Conflict

Any time humans get together, the potential for conflict exists. The chances for conflict multiply as more and more people are added to the mix. Each of us brings our own unique perspectives, backgrounds, and experiences with us to the workplace. We all have different personalities, needs, wants, and histories. There is an assumption that the way we look at things, our perspective, is the way things are. We think that we see clearly, while others may not. We sometimes explain the differences we notice by saying others

Section 6: Managing Conflict in the Workplace

are wrong, stupid, misled, poorly raised, uneducated or any number of other misguided reasons.

We are all different. We have all had different experiences. We all have different values. We all process events differently and think differently. Is it so surprising or shocking that someone could have a different set of priorities about what tasks we should do and when they should be done? Should we be shocked when a coworker makes a joke or tries to be funny, and we just think it's rude? We are all on our own little set of train tracks heading to our own specific destination. It should not surprise us when some of these various tracks cross paths or even occasionally create a head-on collision. What starts out as a slight irritation in a coworker has the potential to morph into an annoyance and then frustration, leading to anger and even rage.

Relationships, Not People, Are Our Most Important Resource

It is often said in business circles, "people are our most important resource." I don't believe it is people, per se. I believe it's the relationships people have that allow them to impact the world.

We accomplish what we accomplish through people, more specifically through our relationships with people. Does any manager want to run the entire front desk by themselves? If not, they will need to bring together a functioning team to accomplish the task.

Two General Types of Work-Related Conflict

There are two general types of work-related conflict. The **first** is interpersonal conflict or differences in personalities. The **second** is work-related or performance-related conflict. Let's talk about interpersonal conflict first.

141

Leadership: Building and Nurturing a World-Class Team of Massage Therapists

Interpersonal Conflict

Interpersonal conflict is a situation where two people fail to get along on a personal level.

They may both be very good at their jobs, but fail to interact well on the personal side of the relationship. They may clash for any number of reasons, including:

- Conflicting values and opinions.
- Different backgrounds and experience levels.
- Different senses of humor. What is funny to one is offensive to the other.

Let's be honest, sometimes people just don't "click." Sometimes personalities just don't mesh well.

This conflict may take the form of overall friction or tension or degenerate into a full-scale battle. Hurt feelings may ensue, causing anger, resentment, and jealousy. These areas of interpersonal conflict may be from words exchanged or some other interaction between them. These interpersonal issues may stay between these two individuals, or the problems can spread to entire groups of team members. Conflict can result in polarization into different groups or factions within the organization.

Workplace Conflict

Workplace conflict arises because of any number of work-related scenarios. Examples might be things like:

- Differing ideas about how to do a particular task.
- Differing ideas about when to do a particular task.
- Differing ideas about who should do a particular task.
- One team member not pulling their weight.
- One team member "bossing" another.

142

Section 6: Managing Conflict in the Workplace

Work-related conflict is directly related to the team members' actual work practices, rather than merely a personality difference. Some work-related disputes can be worked out between team members. Most often, the manager will need to be brought into the discussion as a mediator.

Group Dynamics

At the heart of conflict in the workplace is something referred to as group dynamics. Humans evolved in a group or tribal setting and are genetically tuned to optimize for functioning well in a group or tribal environment. For hundreds of thousands of years, humans' survival was, in large measure, determined by their ability to navigate the complexities of the group. If we were kicked out of the tribe, we risk dying. The work of an early twentieth-century psychologist, Abraham Maslow, helps us understand our relation to a tribe.

Abraham Maslow

Abraham Maslow, a psychologist who did his work from 1930 to 1950, developed a model to explain the scope and importance of various human needs and motivations. His ideas and concepts have application to our discussion here. Maslow's model of human behavior says a human's first priority is to survive. He developed a model based on several basic human needs. He often represented these needs as a pyramid, with the most basic needs at the bottom and the more esoteric or aspirational needs and desires at the top.

At the base of the pyramid are the physical needs we have for survival, such as food, clothing, and shelter. Next is physical safety. After safety, humans seek to belong to a community. These make up the foundation of the pyramid; they form the survival section. (Notice the labels to the left and right of the pyramid)

If humans can take care of survival, the next stage of the pyramid is for humans to thrive. Thriving involves a community, safety, and a feeling of

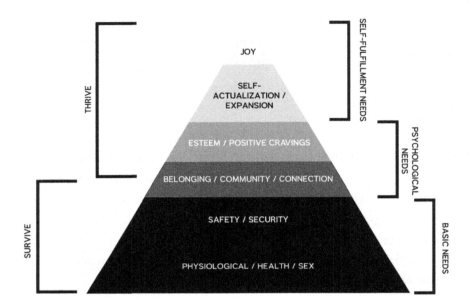

belonging. Self-esteem, or a sense of worth as a person. Self-development or self-actualization, and finally, striving for a state of joy or happiness.

There are several other things to note about Maslow's model. One is the concept of a **perceived threat**. Humans are always on the lookout for threats to our survival. We ask ourselves questions about the people we come into contact with, such as:

- Are they genuine?
- Are they authentic?
- Can I trust them?
- Do they mean me harm?

These questions and concerns are programmed into our DNA. We can't help ourselves from asking the above questions and watching out for a perceived threat.

Section 6: Managing Conflict in the Workplace

Social status is also an important component of group dynamics. The higher a person is on the social status scale, the greater their chances of survival. From the very beginning, humans have been conscience of and worked to move up the social ladder. For this reason, a **perceived slight** or **perceived disrespect** by someone, like a workmate, is registered by humans as a threat to our survival. In the background of our unconscious, we are continually evaluating those around us, asking questions like:

- Do they erode my self-esteem?
- Do they erode my social status?
- Are they a threat to my survival?

The reason for bringing Maslow's Pyramid into the discussion is to demonstrate how seemingly small interpersonal conflict issues can influence some very large and very real human survival instincts. When we understand some of these relationships between current interpersonal interactions and some fundamental human needs, we can make a little more sense of why these things get to us and why we might react as we do. Although based on solid evolutionary biology, many of our reactions have little bearing on our survival in today's world.

Sources of Workplace Conflict

With Maslow's model of human behavior as a foundation, we can now discuss group dynamics in the workplace. As we talk about how conflict arises in the workplace, we will be referring back to the basics of human behavior.

My hope is that many of the challenges found in workplace conflict will be seen through a different lens in light of the above discussion of group dynamics and Maslow's model of human behavior. Let's outline some of the potential sources of interpersonal workplace conflict.

Leadership: Building and Nurturing a World-Class Team of Massage Therapists

1. Lack of trust

One of the sources of workplace conflict is when one team member shares something with others that was meant to be private. Breaches of confidence and the sharing of information without a person's consent is a violation of trust. When we don't feel we can trust someone, it causes an instant question of, "Am I in danger?" The person's very survival feels threatened. Betrayal of confidence between team members becomes a significant source of workplace conflict. Consciously, we might be just angry or have a sense of hurt and sadness. But subconsciously, the reason for the anger and hurt is that, on some level, our very survival is under attack. When this happens, we go into a protective mode. We will have much more to say about trust and its importance later in the book.

2. Feeling isolated

Interpersonal conflict often has a polarizing effect. Workplace conflict can cause various people in the group to take one side of an issue and others to take the opposite side.

When we are isolated from any part of the group, that survival instinct kicks in, and we feel threatened. A couple of examples of how this can manifest itself with co-workers is when people are making plans in front of you and you are not included, or when people have inside jokes and laugh about inside issues when you are present. Be aware of your surroundings when discussing plans and inside jokes and think about how it could lead to someone having feelings of isolation.

3. Passive-aggressive comments

Comments by team members that are often made under the cloak of "just kidding" can create an undercurrent of conflict. When comments are made with a ring of truth to them, we are left to make up a story about the person's intent. Whatever statement is made followed by "just kidding" can sew chords of disharmony and conflict. A good rule of thumb is if you have to say "just kidding" after the statement, you probably shouldn't say it.

146

Section 6: Managing Conflict in the Workplace

4. Different values

We all have different sets of values. These differences can be the source of workplace conflict. Swearing, cursing or perceived lewd comments or jokes can be off putting to some members of the team. Moral choices and dating practices can be very different from person to person. These differences in values can cause some team members to judge and make comments about other team members' behaviors. This has the potential to create hurt feelings and distance between team members.

5. Passing judgment

Related to the above issue of different values is the practice of passing judgment. We do not like it much when other people pass judgment on us. This is because we are aware that other people rarely have the full story of why we do what we do. They usually have no information on our history and the considerations we made that led to our actions and decisions. People often judge us based on minimal information. Yet, we are often very comfortable judging others with the same level of limited information. If we had more information about the person, their history, and the reasons for their actions, it might keep us from reacting and judging the way we do.

6. Lack of tolerance

If you have children, you know how easy it can be to overlook their foibles and idiosyncrasies and focus on their good qualities. It's natural behavior when dealing with our cute and adorable children. We usually have infinitely less tolerance when it comes to the gaffs and missteps of our coworkers.

7. Taking yourself too seriously

If we could lighten up and not take ourselves so seriously, we might feel that we get annoyed much less. If we take ourselves too seriously, we may miss the humor in situations and become offended when none was intended.

8. We allow other people to trigger us

For a situation to progress to anger and rage, a trigger is often involved. We relate this behavior to another behavior in our past that was also a negative experience. I don't know about you, but I really disliked the concept that other people can trigger me. I don't want to give other people that power over me. Through self-reflection and self-discipline, I would hope that I could move out of reactivity and rationally respond to situations around me. I want to develop myself to the point where others will not control my emotions and feelings.

9. Not taking time to understand

Sometimes we rush to conclusions and don't take the time to find out and understand why someone did something. We also don't always take the time to sleep on it. Sometimes we rush to feelings that don't need to be there. If we just wait a few hours before reacting, the situation might resolve itself.

10. Lack of Curiosity

We seldom wonder why others have the positions they have and why they think the way they do. There are many ways to process and think about people who have views different from ours. We can dismiss those with differing opinions, or we can adopt an attitude of curiosity. When we become curious, we try to understand how and why the other person is taking their position. People who are curious ask questions and try to understand the other perspective.

11. Arrogance

If we are not careful and reflective, we can see ourselves as the smartest person in the room, where we see clearly and everyone else is mentally deficient. Arrogance is the opposite of curiosity. Arrogance presupposes that we are always right. And it shuts off the possibility we can learn from those around us.

Section 6: Managing Conflict in the Workplace

12. Creating a story

We often see situations with our co-workers, and without knowing all the details, we create a story. The problem is we create a story based on the limited information we have. We do this often unconsciously. Creating inaccurate stories is often a source of conflict. We will explore this idea in much greater detail in another section of this book

13. Gossip

Gossiping brings a devastating force to teams. High-Performing teams keep gossiping to a minimum.

Let's refer to the Oak Haven Way card, behavior # 6:

> Help build up, support, and inspire fellow team members.
> Refrain from gossiping. Let's inspire and make a difference
> in the lives of our coworkers by helping them reach their
> full potential.

Oak Haven Massage is a no gossip zone. Each team member signs an agreement when they come aboard. It looks something like this:

Gossip Policy Agreement

When light conversation changes into comments about a person who is not present that are negative or intending to incite anger or "choose sides," it has become gossip. If it causes conflict or negativity or hurts the person who is being spoken of, it's gossip.

Sometimes even a seemingly harmless venting session can get blown out of proportion if the topics expressed get passed from person to person.

Gossip is a toxic behavior and activity. It usually stems from misinformation, like a bad game of telephone; the further from the source, the more warped the information gets. It hurts people's feelings and can ultimately

Leadership: Building and Nurturing a World-Class Team of Massage Therapists

affect morale and the overall attitude of the workplace. It damages trust between coworkers and can trigger anxiety and tension.

Oak Haven Massage has worked hard to develop a culture that holds integrity, honesty, teamwork, and a positive work environment in high regard. But management can only do so much to help foster these attitudes. We need YOUR help.

- If a coworker is speaking negatively about another coworker or sharing personal information about a coworker who is not present, please do not engage.
- If you feel the need to vent or voice a grievance, please do so to management. Your manager is the one who can listen (if an ear is all you're looking for) or the one who can work to help you solve the problem.

Joining the Oak Haven Massage team means that you commit to creating a positive work environment by not engaging in gossip.

_____   _____

Signature   Date

Gossiping is defined as **communication among team members focused on the private, personal, and sensitive affairs of others who are not present.**

Gossip is often malicious in nature and serves no beneficial purpose. We ask you to avoid gossip at all costs. Gossip, uncontrolled, can be very damaging to fellow team members.

How do you tell the difference between idle chat and gossip? Consider the words of Mary Abbajay on this issue:

> While idle chit-chat and other light conversation can be value-neutral, gossip is often negative, inflammatory, and

Section 6: Managing Conflict in the Workplace

embarrassing to the person being spoken about. Here is a test. Consider the impact of what is being said. Does it cast negative aspersions? Does it create riffs? Does it exult in the misfortune of others? Does it have a negative emotional charge? Does it serve to perpetuate conflict or negativity? Is it hurtful or damaging? Is it something you would say in front of that person?

Gossip is hurtful and can destroy trust among team members. It also has a devastating effect on employee morale.

How to Help Decrease Workplace Gossip

It's important to realize that gossiping requires two people: the gossiper and the person listening to the gossip. If you actively listen to gossip, you are a co-promoter of gossip in the workplace. The more you listen, the more you encourage it. If you don't listen, gossip cannot happen. Here are some things you can do to decrease the spreading of gossip in the workplace

Don't participate. Walk away or give visual cues you're not interested. In a recent article, Pamela Hawley, founder and CEO of Universal Giving, shared one of my favorite Stephen Covey quotes:

> One of the most important ways to manifest integrity is to be loyal to those who are not present. In doing so, we build the trust of those who are present. When you defend those who are absent, you retain the trust of those present.

Hawley went on to say:

> How easy it is to slight the person who slighted you? Maybe you were kinder, but you still wanted *to do that little jab back*. No matter what someone has done to you, you can take a stand for goodness. You can take a stand for integrity.

151

As Stephen Covey, one of our greatest leadership writers, admonishes us, if you want to demonstrate true integrity, "Be loyal to those not present." What does it mean if you speak negatively of a person when they're not present? You're doing it for your own ego, your own self-satisfaction, and building up your own sense of "justice." Do you really think making disparaging comments about others is going to lift you up? It won't. In fact, it's going to tear you down. If you try to pull others down, you pull yourself down with them. Being loyal to those not present builds trust. What Stephen Covey is saying is, be gracious. Uphold others' character—and your own character—by speaking well of others, especially when they are not present.

Another way to help decrease workplace gossip is to turn it around by saying something positive about the person. You can also completely change the subject to a non-gossip topic. Make sure you can recognize the difference between venting and gossiping. Often, there is not a lot of difference, and it may just be a matter of intent. You can also offer another perspective (i.e., "Maybe they didn't mean it that way...").

Gossip often involves some or many of the following:

- I know something you don't. It gives us a bit of a thrill to know things that others do not know.
- Gossiping is often a way of bonding with the person you're sharing with.
- Gossiping is often seen as nothing harmless, just a way of sharing information.
- Gossiping is often a way of building your own team. It's a way of creating our own little posse. We are gathering our forces. It's a war, and we need to recruit all the folks we can.

Section 6: Managing Conflict in the Workplace

- It's a way to stir the pot. Some people like to stir things up. Some people think a drama-free environment is boring.

Gossip does not always have a sinister purpose, but it always has a negative impact on the team. Even if it's that the person you shared information with no longer trusts you because they wonder what you are saying behind their back.

If it's not true, helpful, inspiring, necessary, and/or kind, don't say it.

If you have the digital version of this book, you can click the link below to hear an excellent five-minute discussion on honest conversations workplace gossip by Scott Miller in an interview on StoryBrand.

https://soundcloud.com/user-166537898/honest-conversations-gossip

Venting

Sometimes a coworker feels the need to get something off their chest. Occasionally, a fellow team member will tell you about a person or a situation that has them frustrated. They are venting. Letting off some steam. Sometimes, all you need to do in a situation like this is listen to the other person. Sometimes the person just needs to be heard. Often, just the process of talking about an issue makes the situation a little more bearable. We make a distinction between gossip and venting. Gossip involves the private, personal affairs of others and is often malicious in its intent. Venting more often involves a situation that has developed and is frustrating to the individual.

Most of us have engaged in venting at some point in our lives.

153

The Power of Awareness

I don't necessarily have any solutions at this point on how we might avoid these areas of workplace conflict. My purpose here is to point out the various ways conflict can occur and examine the sources. It's possible that just being aware of how conflict arises will help us to minimize it. As we 2gain a better understanding of how we are all different and how we all have different lenses through which we see the world, it can make us more aware of the need to keep confidence, avoid gossip, and be more inclusive with team members.

Is it Essential That We Like Our Coworkers?

Here is an interesting question: Do we have to like our co-workers?

I would say we don't necessarily have to like or love our coworkers. Although both liking them and loving them are a great benefit to work-related harmony. If we can't like or love our coworkers, we can, at the very least, learn to respect and tolerate them. We can also learn to appreciate the contribution they make to the team. Maybe we can even commit to a peaceful co-existence.

When we are not wasting our efforts on strife and disharmony, we can focus on serving the customer's needs, which ultimately leads to your own professional success and happiness.

We Don't Usually Get to Choose Our Coworkers

Coworkers are like family. We don't get to choose our family. Unless we are a manager who hires, we generally don't get to pick our coworkers. Because of this, it becomes critical that we gain tools to manage and resolve conflict. We can't walk away from coworkers (unless we quit or leave the business) any more than we can walk away from a sibling or parent. Just like in a family, conflict and discord can creep in, and we need to find a way to navigate it.

Section 6: Managing Conflict in the Workplace

Ideas for Minimizing Workplace Conflict

Sometimes we need to make structural changes to the workplace to minimize conflict. One thing we could do to reduce workplace conflict is have better training. Some conflict is related to confusion regarding the duties of the front desk. If we had well-established procedures and priorities for front desk team members, this would help keep individual members from establishing their own preferences. More complete training could help to minimize conflict.

We could also have more practice and training related to peer-to-peer conflict resolution. This would help with the willingness to engage in honest conversations.

Team members could benefit from training regarding when it's appropriate to speak with a coworker about an issue. It can be challenging to know when to bring an issue to a coworker's attention or when to involve the manager.

We could have training about what issues require a manager to be involved. Some problems can be resolved easily and quickly by team members talking it out. Some issues are inherently more complicated and will require a manager to be involved. It would be helpful for training to occur as to which problems require a manager's involvement.

It might be useful if managers were trained to bring together both team members when interpersonal issues become problematic. Rather than listen to one team member tell their side of the story.

Training so team members better understand the peer review process and how it allows them to rate and evaluate coworkers could also be useful.

Personal Development as a Tool for Minimizing Work-Related Conflict

What can each of us as team members do to better prepare ourselves to lessen workplace conflict? The following are a few things that we can do to work on ourselves in this important area. If you think about it, we only really have control over ourselves. This seems like a logical place to start as we deal with workplace conflict.

Lessons from Victor Frankel

Victor Frankel was a Jewish psychiatrist from Austria who was captured by the Nazis in World War II. Over three years, from 1942 to 1945, he was in four different concentration camps.

During his time in the concentration camps, Victor Frankel experienced horrors that would be unimaginable to people living today. His parents, brother, and wife all died in the camps. His sister was the only survivor. Victor Frankel spent three years never knowing what his fate would be. He came to some significant insights during that time. He realized that no matter his situation, no matter how atrocious or hopeless, he still had the power to choose how he would respond. His Nazi captures could treat him in ruthless and horrible ways. Still, he had one final freedom he determined could never be taken away from him—the freedom to choose his response to the situation. Frankel wrote a book about his experience in the camps entitled *Man's Search for Meaning*. This book had an immediate impact when released in 1946 and has continued to be on bestseller lists today. Amazon rates it as "One of the 100 books to read in your lifetime." In it, Frankel describes his harrowing experience in the Nazi death camps. One of the great quotes from the book is: "Everything can be taken from a man but one thing, the last of human freedoms, to choose one's attitude in any given set of circumstances, to choose one's own way."

We will come back to Victor Frankel's insights. Let's build on this concept of freedom to choose with a discussion on stimulus and response.

Understanding Stimulus and Response

The phrase, "He made me mad," is something we might hear as we go through our life. Someone making you mad is an example of the concept of stimulus and response. It might be diagramed this way.

Section 6: Managing Conflict in the Workplace

Someone does something, says something, or implies something, and it causes us to get mad. You will notice in the graphic there is an arrow between the stimulus and response. The arrow represents a gap, a period of time between the event (stimulus) and the reaction to the event (response). This period of time after the stimulus is what Victor Frankel was referring to when he said everything can be taken from a man (or woman) but one thing, the last of human freedoms, to choose one's attitude in any given set of circumstances.

In the gap, the period following a life event (stimulus), we have a very uniquely human opportunity. During this time, we can choose the way we respond. Humans are endowed with a quality that allows us to choose between multiple options. We don't have to be at the mercy of a pre-programmed conditioned response.

In his book *The 7 Habits of Highly Effective People*, Stephen Covey speaks of the human ability to exercise an "independent will." Covey speaks of the unique human quality of self-awareness, a quality that separates humans from all other forms of life on earth.

It's our self-awareness, our independent will, and our ultimate freedom of choice that allows us to have the options Frankel spoke of.

When a stimulus (event) is presented to us, we have a couple of options. We can respond, or we can react.

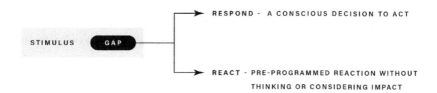

Leadership: Building and Nurturing a World-Class Team of Massage Therapists

The Gap

The gap, this period of time between a stimulus and our response, is where humans exercise several of the unique qualities just mentioned—self-awareness, independent will, and freedom to choose.

This idea that we choose how to respond to events around us can be a liberating notion or it can be a little disorienting. Stephen Covey states:

> "Between stimulus and response is our greatest power, and the freedom to choose. Our behavior is a function of our decisions, not our situation. People who understand this do not blame their behavior on the circumstances; they know their behavior is a result of their own conscious choice."

To think we all choose our response to situations puts a lot of the responsibility for actions back on us. If you think about it, this kind of crushes the notion of, "He made me mad."

If we agree with Victor Frankel, we would need to rethink the statement, "He made me mad."

Frankel would argue that the last of human freedoms is to choose one's path in any given situation.

With this information about how humans process information, the more accurate statement might be, "He did something, and I chose to be mad."

Luckily, others don't get to choose how we respond to a situation; that is the last of human freedoms that no one can take away from us.

First, Understand That We Choose to be Upset

This is a powerful frame of mind—the realization that anytime we are upset, it's because we chose to be upset. We could just as easily choose to let the issue go. Try this the next time someone does something to upset you. Have an internal talk with yourself. Remind yourself that you have a choice in this matter. No rule states that you must be upset, angry, and frustrated because somebody does something inappropriate. As Stephen Covey says, "It's not what happens to us, but our response to what happens to us that hurts us."

Second, Practice Not Being Offended

What if each of us was a little less thin-skinned? What if we were not so quick to be offended by what others do? Just because a difficult team member does something rude, careless, or thoughtless, we don't have to respond in kind. It's not required that we tell everyone else on the team how we have been wronged. What if we were more like the proverbial duck, who just lets the water runoff its back?

Act Rather Than React

Work towards becoming a person who acts rather than reacts. Stephen Covey has another concept in his *7 Habits* book. He asserts that humans have the capacity to act rather than be acted upon by our circumstances. This might be diagrammed like this.

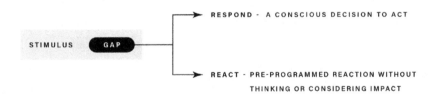

The idea here is that when we act, we are exercising our free will. When we are acted upon, we are victims of circumstances or the situation we find ourselves in. This was Victor Frankel's key insight—humans don't have to let circumstances dictate their response. Humans have the ability to act independently of difficult, even horrible circumstances.

Extending the Gap

One key to acting in a challenging situation versus reacting is to understand the gap.

The gap is a specific length of time. Often in reactive individuals, the gap length is very short, nanoseconds, between a stimulus and the response. It should be comforting to know that the gap length is not set in stone. We can, and should, seek to extend the gap length. It's almost always better to have more time between the event and our response. As I've grown older, I've learned to extend this gap length as long as I need to. I will often sleep on it.

There are times in my life when I'm presented with a situation that initially might cause me to feel upset or even angry. I've learned to recognize this, and, in the spirit of extending the gap, I might choose to take no action right now but sleep on it. It's absolutely amazing what can happen to a supercharged issue when given the perspective of twenty-four hours and a good night's sleep. I've found that my decisions in situations like this are often much better than if I had made the decision immediately.

Some folks are so tightly wound that there is almost no perceptible delay between an event and response. We call this having a pre-programmed response. This type of person is nearly always in a reactive mode. An interesting point is that people in this full reactive mode do not see what is happening. It's almost as if they are a victim, with no control over their responses.

These people in full reactive mode know they are easily upset, but they think it's the stimulus (what the person is doing or saying) that causes their response. They are oblivious to the fact that there is a gap, and they

Section 6: Managing Conflict in the Workplace

have the power to decide how they will respond. It is a useful exercise to remind ourselves that we always have a choice as to how we will react to any given situation.

Work/Performance-Related Conflict

We now venture into a different category of potential conflict. This is when a team member perceives another team member is impacting the business or the customer experience negatively. When a team member feels that another team member is not holding up their end of the workload, resentment and/or conflict may ensue.

This category may involve:

- A team member not pulling their share of the load, such as phones, laundry, and cleaning.
- Bringing personal issues into the workplace.
- Showing up late for shifts.
- Complaining.
- Being critical of coworkers.
- Spending too much time on personal phones or social media.
- A lack of skill sets or making mistakes, and more training is needed.
- Talking with therapists while you do the work or wander off, leaving you to wonder where he/she went.
- Calling out or missing work.
- Not being perceived as a team player.
- Taking his/her shifts when you can, but he/she does not reciprocate.
- Unwillingness to communicate with other team members.
- Not cleaning up after themselves.

The list could go on...

161

Leadership: Building and Nurturing a World-Class Team of Massage Therapists

Confrontation

It's tempting to think that conflict resolution and conflict management is easy. Simply go to the team member you are having issues with and let them know, talk it out. What could go wrong? Well, it turns out, lots of stuff can go wrong.

Many people, around 80 percent, are not comfortable with confrontation. These 80 percent will most likely never initiate a discussion of a problem or issue in the first place. You may be one of the 20 percent who are comfortable with raising an issue with a coworker. It is essential to realize it may very well be an uncomfortable conversation for the non-confrontational team member. Bringing up issues with these non-confrontational team members may end up causing even more problems, hurt feelings, and resentment.

Any confrontation has the potential to raise defensiveness. Many people are highly defensive. Most people see themselves as having the right or correct perspective. Most people have reasons for what they do. Most people want to be right rather than wrong. Most people will try to convince you to see things their way versus being curious and seeing your perspective.

Common Myths About Workplace Conflict

1. **Myth**: Conflict is always negative and should be avoided at work.
    Fact: Conflict is a natural part of human interaction.
2. **Myth**: Difficult people are almost always the cause of conflict.
    Fact: It can and does come from all team members.
3. **Myth**: The problem at the root of conflict is usually obvious.
    Fact: Sometimes it is obvious, sometimes it takes some real investigation to get to the source of the issue.
4. **Myth**: In conflict, there are always winners and losers.
    Fact: If it's done right, conflict resolution can have a win-win situation.
5. **Myth**: It's a manager's responsibility to fix problems on his or her team.

Section 6: Managing Conflict in the Workplace

> **Fact**: Ultimately, team members can resolve many issues on their own.

6. **Myth:** Conflict will do permanent damage that may never be resolved.

    Fact: If a conflict is handled correctly, two people can be closer after the incident than before.

We have an entire section coming up in this book on honest conversation. I will give you many ideas on how to engage in productive discussions with your coworkers.

Not All People are Right for the Team

Okay, let's talk about this, because I'm sure it's crossed your mind. Some team members come on board and they really are rude, insensitive, disrespectful, unhappy, complainers, gossip prone, and lazy.

It's possible that someone interviewed really well. The manager thought they would be a good fit, and it turned out to be the wrong fit. If this happens, you will have ample opportunities to express your thoughts and opinions through your meetings with the manager. We want you to be honest in your assessment and evaluation of who are appropriate team members and who are not. What should not happen is you sowing discord among other staff members to bring others to your way of thinking. We call this gossip and/or pot-stirring, and it will never get you the result you want. Always take your concerns directly to the managers. This is the appropriate way to voice your concerns. Gossiping is not appropriate. Allow the rude, insensitive people to show their true colors. Avoid going on a campaign to rid the team of a perceived menace.

163

The Role of Team Members in Deciding Who Is and Is Not a Good Fit

Managers must realize that team members act differently in the manager's presence than when the manager is not around. It took me many years to realize this. Thus, managers don't always have an accurate picture of the different team members' contributions.

Here we come to a critical discussion related to **culture**. The general culture (how we do things around here) will play a large part in how team members approach these performance-related problems.

Another issue is **training**. Have team members been trained on what to do if a team member is unable or unwilling to adequately perform the job duties?

The perceived **commitment** of the manager in establishing a high-functioning team will also be a factor. If team members think the manager is serious in developing a high-level team, they are more likely to come forward with issues. If they believe the talk of "high level" is just lip service, they may save themselves the trouble and be quiet.

Indeed, the **personality** of the team member who notices problems is a factor. They may not be the type of person who has any level of willingness to go out on a limb to report an issue.

It should be noted that, for anyone, it takes a significant level of **courage** (and regard for the manager and the business) to come forward with an issue. They pay the manager and the company a massive compliment by showing their willingness to risk sounding like a tattletale or complainer. Let's not forget that coming forward with issues is always a risk in team members' eyes. There are many different ways coming forward with issues can come back to bite them. A lot of that depends on the culture of the workplace you are in.

Another Note

Sometimes team members will hesitate to come forward with issues regarding other team members. They think coming forward will get the person

Section 6: Managing Conflict in the Workplace

fired. Team members who have this concern fail to consider the **enormous commitment we have to the people we bring aboard**. They have often been selected from a very large pool of applicants. We are not quick to give up on these folks. Our first reflex is to train and inform—"This is what we need from you. This is how we operate here." Remember, the new hires have been through weeks and possibly months of training at this point at a very high cost to the business. We are going to make every effort to make this work. Any comments you make will help us guide the person towards a path that will allow them to be a contributing member of the team. It also helps us get a full picture of what is going on. If multiple people come forward with the same issue, it helps us understand the severity of the situation. It also brings the manager one step closer to resolving the issue.

Conflict and the Management Team

Conflict Continuum

This next bit of info comes from the book *The Advantage* by Patrick Lencioni. He supports the concept that the right kind of conflict is essential for a high functioning team.

Conflict is usually thought of as something to minimize and control between team members. However, when it comes to the management team, conflict plays an important role. In this context, we don't try to eradicate conflict, but encourage a "healthy" type of conflict. When we use the term "conflict" in this context, we refer to team members being allowed to disagree with upper management and other co-workers and "speak their mind" without fear of any retaliation. If management teams are not able to speak freely, the wisdom of the team is not fully "tapped." The best decisions come as the entire group has an opportunity to weigh in, share opinions openly, and speak their mind freely.

During important management discussions, the fear of conflict or expressing your opinions freely is almost always a sign of problems. At the center of creating healthy conflict is trust.

"When team members trust one another, when they know that everyone on the team is capable of admitting when they don't have the right answer, and when they're willing to acknowledge when someone else's idea is better than theirs, the fear of conflict and the discomfort it entails, is greatly diminished. When there is trust, conflict becomes nothing more than the pursuit of truth, simply an attempt to find the best possible answer."
—Patrick Lencioni

This doesn't mean that even "healthy" conflict isn't a little uncomfortable.

"Overcoming the tendency to run from discomfort is one of the most important requirements for any leadership team—in fact, for any leader."
—Patrick Lencioni

A useful concept taught by Lencioni is the conflict continuum. He explains this concept as follows:

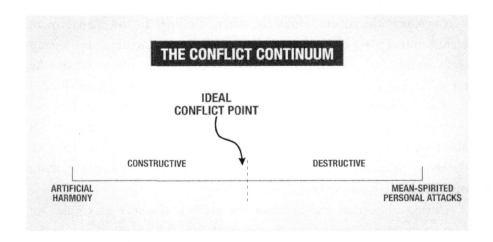

Section 6: Managing Conflict in the Workplace

"At one end of the continuum is no conflict at all. I call this artificial harmony because it is marked by a lot of false smiling and disingenuous agreement around just about everything, at least publicly. At the other end of the continuum is relentless, nasty, and destructive conflict, with people constantly at one another's throats. As you move away from the extreme of artificial harmony, you encounter more and more constructive conflict. Somewhere in the middle of these two extremes is the demarcation line where good, constructive conflict crosses over into the destructive kind.

"Most organizations live somewhere fairly close to the artificial harmony end of this continuum. They go out of their way to avoid direct, uncomfortable disagreement during meetings or doing anything that would suggest moving away from their comfortable end of the scale. Why? Because whenever they move down the line toward the middle, to that place where they're having more and more constructive conflict, they seem themselves one step closer to conflict Armageddon. So, they run back to the world of passive, indirect communication and artificial agreement. The optimal place to be on the continuum is just to the left of the demarcation line. That would be the point where a team is engaged in all the constructive conflict they could possibly have but never stepping over the line into destructive territory. Of course, this is impossible. In any team, and for that matter, in any family or marriage, someone at some point is going to step over the line and say or do something that isn't constructive. But rather than fearing this, teams need to accept that it will happen and learn to manage it. They must be willing to live through

167

Leadership: Building and Nurturing a World-Class Team of Massage Therapists

the messiness of recovering from slightly inappropriate conflict, so that they will have the courage to go back to the best place again and again. Eventually, they'll develop the confidence that they can survive an occasional step over the line and can even get stronger and build greater trust with one another when they do."

—Patrick Lencioni

Healthy Conflict

So, it can be good to have some healthy conflict within a group. Now, how do you encourage healthy conflict? Conflict, any conflict, can be considered confrontational. And many people are not comfortable with confrontation. However, it all goes back to trust. We need to trust that our team members and leadership team have our back. We need to trust that they are only bringing something to our attention to make the business better. It would help to recognize that we don't have to be offended. If we are all on the same page on this, we can have a healthy dialogue about the best possible course of action.

Management's role is to set the vision and direction of the company and to manage the affairs of the business in the best possible way. All members of the management team and the entire Oak Haven team should feel free to voice their opinions on topics that arise in a management meeting. I know this sounds like I'm stating the obvious, but contrary to what you might think, many members of the management team will feel uncomfortable voicing an opposing view to a plan or direction that the general manager or CEO may be recommending.

It's all about threats and taking risks. When someone expresses an opinion contrary to the group, if the culture is not one of openness and receptivity, the dissenter runs the risk of being labeled a troublemaker, a rebel rouser, or worse. His or her status in the hierarchy of the social group work structure is potentially threatened, and, ultimately, their livelihood is

Section 6: Managing Conflict in the Workplace

at risk. As silly as this issue might sound to us right now (we are in a calm environment having a civil discussion), in the heat of a strategy meeting with all the emotion flowing, it is a genuine concern for many. The leader of any meeting sets the tone for what is and is not acceptable in terms of dissension or voicing an opposing opinion.

If a plan is presented as:

> "We've thought this out, and here is what we are going to do. Here is the thought process that we went through; here are the questions that came up. Here is how we propose we deal with these issues. We think this is a brilliant plan. Who is with us?"

> Crickets.

> "Great, let's do it."

Let's look at what just happened. The leader did not set the stage for any level of pushback. The leader did not ask for alternative views or what problems anyone could see with the proposal. Anyone who questions in this environment will likely be shut down and told to get on board. What if the CEO had come into the meeting with a completely open mind? What might have happened if the CEO explained and set forth the issues, then asked for possible solutions? Is it possible the conversation might have gone another way?

It's possible that a very valuable and insightful discussion would have ensued. It is also possible that the CEO may have heard some ideas that were not previously entertained. In situations like this, it's imperative that the leader of the group speak last and render his or her opinions at the end of their discussion rather than at the beginning. This way, the potential to bias the group is minimized. This is a topic that could easily fit under the category of culture because that really is the issue here. It's critical that, as leaders, we establish a culture of freedom of expression and openness to ideas. Doesn't it make sense that the people who are to be tasked with the implementation of whatever plan is approved should have significant input in the final decision?

Team members must feel they can push back on ideas without the fear of being shut down or marginalized. The CEO or leader must go into these types of meetings with a mental framework of, "I have no idea what will come out of this meeting or what direction we will ultimately go, but I trust the wisdom of our team, and I have confidence we can get it right."

If the leader has this attitude, a lively, spirited discussion or series of discussions is possible, and a workable plan is likely to be born.

If you have the digital version of this book, you can listen to an excellent podcast on healthy workplace conflict here with Patrick Lencioni.

https://podcasts.apple.com/us/podcast/at-the-table-with-patrick-lencioni/id1474171732?i=1000446318933

Be the Last to Speak

Simon Sinek – Great Video – 2 minutes

https://www.inc.com/jessica-stillman/5-little-words-that-will-make-you-a-much-better-le.html

Reward Dissent

Create a workplace culture where it's okay to disagree, even strongly in closed meetings, but fully support whatever decisions are made in public.

Patrick Lencioni makes the observation: "If someone were to offer me one single piece of evidence to evaluate the health of an organization, I would want to observe the leadership team during a meeting."

Is there vigorous debate and respectful disagreement, or does everyone weakly fall in line with the leader, terrified of backlash from voicing a differing opinion?

If you are building a team anywhere in your life or business, ask yourself, "Am I looking to surround myself with the most capable men and

Section 6: Managing Conflict in the Workplace

women? Or am I looking for people who just agree with whatever I want to recommend?"

> "Exemplary leaders reward dissent. They encourage it. They understand that, whatever momentary discomfort they experience as a result of being told they might be wrong, it is more than offset by the fact that the information will help them make better decisions."
>
> —Warren Bennis

We want to create an environment where the team has full freedom to disagree, argue, and persuade the group to his or her way of thinking… hopefully within the parameters of the conflict continuum. With practice and effort, passionate discussion can take place without crossing over the line into destructive conflict.

Then, when the battle is over and the decision is made, the dynamic changes, a switch occurs; the management team goes into full unity mode. There are no more camps, no more persuading, that time has passed. No throwing people under the bus—"I didn't want this, but Bill got his way." You move forward and give your full effort and allegiance to the working of the plan that was decided upon. Once the decision is made, we are ONE.

It's acceptable to re-visit, with the management team, things we feel strongly about. Sometimes it takes time to get others to "see the light." But this is done in the relative privacy of a management team meeting. It is not done in open rebellion in front of the team.

Advisory Committees

Leaders and managers ultimately want to make the best decisions possible for the customer, the team, and the business. Having open and honest discussions with the leadership team is one way to arrive at the best decision

Leadership: Building and Nurturing a World-Class Team of Massage Therapists

possible. Another way to gain valuable insight into issues facing the business is by the establishment of advisory committees.

An advisory committee is a select group of trusted team members who are asked to attend either one meeting or a series of meetings to solve a specific problem. The committee is comprised of four to ten people who are familiar with the issues involved and/or may be affected by the decision.

Committee members are generally chosen for any number of reasons, including:

- They are willing to be open, honest, and direct.
- They have specific knowledge of the issue or problem being discussed.
- They are trusted members of the Oak Haven team, and they are familiar with the culture and mission of Oak Haven.
- Management values their wisdom and judgment.
- They are in a position to represent the interests of the larger group.

These committees are not permanent. They are formed as needed and then disbanded. If other issues come up, and an advisory committee is required again, another committee is selected. The new committee may have team members on it who have already served before, or it may not. I like the idea of allowing a wide variety of team members to participate in this process. So, I try to be as inclusive as possible and invite new people to be a part of these committees as they are formed. I will often ask one or two experienced, trusted team members to participate as well. Individual schedules are often conflicting, and not everyone we invite can attend. Committee members are paid an hourly rate for their participation on the committee. Depending on the topic, we often ask for volunteers who would want to give honest feedback.

It's possible to use an advisory committee successfully in a number of different ways. I will outline my personal preferences here.

Section 6: Managing Conflict in the Workplace

I like to spend time with an idea or problem on my own before meeting with the advisory committee. I may wrestle with an issue for several weeks or several months before setting up the committee. I may speak with several people as part of my research and pre-committee work. I will certainly speak with managers about the issue or issues involved. I will often have one or two possible solutions to the problem to present to the group. Even though I have done extensive thinking and research into the issue at hand, I am careful not to put forward any ideas to the group early on. I don't want to influence the group with my thoughts too soon in the process. The important part here is that I'm not going into the advisory committee meeting totally unprepared. I have spent lots of time thinking and preparing.

I like to set aside at least two hours for these meetings. Sometimes as many as three hours. It can take a while to debate and to get to the heart of the matter. Depending on how far we get, we may schedule one or two follow-up meetings.

Set the Stage for Discussion

First, set the stage for the discussion. Let the group know you want their honest opinions. Let them know you want to approach this issue from a brainstorming perspective, which means there are no bad ideas. Often, the crazier, the better. Another point to handle at the start of the meeting is to set expectations about how the decision at hand will be made.

A Note About How Decisions are Made

Nearly always, when important decisions need to be made, we get together a group of managers or call together an advisory committee. The purpose of these groups is to get input before the decision is made. We are attempting to tap into the collective brain trust of the group in the hope of making a more informed and ultimately better decision.

I spent the last several pages outlining the need for members of these groups to be as honest and open as possible. I encouraged managers and

173

Leadership: Building and Nurturing a World-Class Team of Massage Therapists

other leaders to keep their opinions to themselves, at least initially, to keep from influencing the group to their way of thinking.

I also brought up the principle that once the decision is made, the decision is over, and we move forward as one, united in executing the decision. But I want to be clear from the very start about how the decision is made. It is most often the manager, the president of the company, or possibly even the owners who make the final decision, based on an assortment of input and opinions. The final decision is not usually a vote. Business is not a democracy. I share this because sometimes, members of an advisory committee will feel strongly about a particular issue. They might advocate very powerfully for a specific course of action. If the decision goes contrary to their desires, they might feel slighted or even feel as though their opinion did not matter. It is important to go into these meetings willing to share your viewpoints but knowing that leadership will make the final decision based on many factors. Some issues you may not even be aware of due to privacy issues. The advisory committee member's task is to get their opinion and all the facts out in the open, so the best possible decision can be made. If the decision goes against what a committee member wanted, it's important that they get on board and help to make the decision a success.

Four Methods to Approaching the Decision–Making Process

1. Command or decree

This method is like a kingdom, a command or decree may be given. Here, there is no consultation. The leader ponders an issue and comes up with what they think will be the best solution. Once the decision has been made, the leader will announce it to the organization.

2. Vote

This is where the issue is outlined, options are discussed, then a group of people will vote. It's a democracy.

174

Section 6: Managing Conflict in the Workplace

3. Consensus

With this method, the group making the decision will talk and discuss until everyone or a majority of the group agree as to the path forward.

4. Consultative Approach

With a consultative approach, the leader invites others to weigh in on the issue or problem. The leader is attempting to gain information, insight, and understanding as well as ideas for solutions. With this approach, the leader will ask for discussion and input from a group before making the final decision.

Set Expectations

At the beginning of the advisory meeting, be sure to outline how this committee is being used. And how the final decision will be made. In most cases, we use the advisory committee in a consultative way. The leaders are looking for input and discussion. They will then weigh the different options and make a final decision. The committee may not even be aware of the final decision until it is announced to the entire team.

This issue of outlining how the final decision will be made is an essential part of setting the committee's initial parameters.

Outline the Problem or Issue

I see the committee function as twofold. One is to generate ideas and possible solutions to the problem at hand. The second is to ratify or approve a possible solution. This process can be very useful in both of these areas depending on the nature of the issue involved. Decide in advance what the purpose of the committee is. Is it to assist leadership in finding a solution? Or is the committee's function to understand the nature of the problem or issue, listen to a possible solution proposed by management, and weigh in on the workability of the proposed solution? I have used advisory

175

Leadership: Building and Nurturing a World-Class Team of Massage Therapists

committees effectively for both of these approaches. I have come to an advisory committee with a problem and a proposed solution. And the committee has shot me down without mercy. I went back to the drawing board and attempted to come up with a more workable idea. Then came back to the committee for additional input.

Regardless of the exact reason you have established the committee, it is important to go into the meeting with an open mind. If you are not open to the group's ideas, don't form the committee in the first place. If you're not open to new ideas, just announce the problem and your solution in a company-wide meeting and be done with the matter. The use of advisory committees has been a key factor in establishing the culture of Oak Haven Massage. Team members feel valued when they are included in these important decisions that have the potential to affect them. They always have important insights into the problems, and they understand the potential implications of different possible solutions.

We often have long-standing employees on the committee, those who have been with our company since the beginning. As these people understand the issues and help develop solutions, it gives them buy-in to whatever solutions or decisions are eventually made. These key members are then able to influence other members of the team and show support for the decision.

Change is often difficult. It is helpful to have as many team members as possible understand the issues at a deeper level. It's helpful if team members know the process and thinking that went into making the final decision.

Cultivate Confrontation

Click the link below for an excellent three-minute discussion on cultivating confrontation.

https://soundcloud.com/user-166537898/leadership-confrontation

Section 6: Managing Conflict in the Workplace

Three Dangers of Conflict Avoidance. Are You Suffering from Any? Or All?

By Rick Houcek

Uh-oh, I've already got the "conflict avoiders" quaking in their boots, just reading that headline. Conflict is something an avoider hates, prefers to ignore, and would rather have a root canal than engage in a difficult discussion. But wait, let's back up... and first define it. Conflict—as seen by most—involves anger, ugly yelling, uncomfortable disagreement, elevated blood pressure, clenched fists, and sometimes gets physical. That, in reality, is a very small minority of cases. Extremely small. Fact is, each of us deals with conflict multiple times a day, over very safe, benign, non-threatening subjects. And yet, many still panic and bailout. It could be as harmless as a husband and wife discussing what movie to go see, and each has a different preference. Or, football coaches deciding the next play but not agreeing. Or a business team struggling with a strategic move and can't reach consensus. None of which need be perilous or nasty.

Here's my definition of conflict: It's when two or more people are discussing a subject, any subject, and they have different opinions and disagree on what action to take. Period. Nothing more ugly or heinous or dreadful than that. It doesn't have to involve screaming, name-calling, or fistfights. In fact, when I lead high-stakes strategic planning retreats with aggressive-growth companies, I establish "rules of engagement" up front, so leadership team discussions are dignified and respectful—yet still tackle tough, thorny subjects and arrive at unified decisions. So far, it's worked every time without bloodshed, and I've led 364 multi-day planning retreats over twenty-six years. In each one, there have been TONS of disagreement as discussions begin, then as we weigh different options, examine pros and cons, hear all viewpoints...we eventually reach

Leadership: Building and Nurturing a World-Class Team of Massage Therapists

a unified position of team buy-in. And no one died. No one threw a punch. No one got insulted or demeaned. No one. Ever.

My wife and I even have what we call "rules for disagreeing" that we established before we got married. The happy result is, while we don't always see eye-to-eye—we never fight—and have an incredible, respectful, loving marriage. And we never end a disagreement angry. Yes, it's doable. As author and preacher Max Lucado brilliantly stated, "Conflict is unavoidable. Combat is optional."

So, if you have disagreements with important people in your life—and who doesn't?—then you have a choice: Respectful, dignified conflict? Or irate, devastating combat? I'll opt for the former every time. And I won't run and hide from the discussion.

Bottom line: Here are three dangers of conflict avoidance.

1. You'll never get what you want, and you'll be miserable. If you always acquiesce, always back down, don't speak up, never engage in the discussion…then how can you expect to ever get what you really want? When this happens in a two-person discussion, one person always has the power—and it's not you. By avoiding, you've lost. Worse, you'll get angry at the other person for "always getting his way"—when, in fairness, it's your fault, not hers. You gave up.

2. You risk settling for an inferior decision. The best decisions often start with multiple options—not just one—and much disagreement. When two or five or eight different views are shared among decision-makers, the final decision is often none of them—but a new option that is better than all—borne out of the discussion—and perhaps even a blending of several original options. But if you avoid conflict—and don't have the discussion—you'll never know how good it could have been—and your final decision will be a lower grade choice.

Section 6: Managing Conflict in the Workplace

3. You don't advance the relationship. Relationships between individuals or between team members are strengthened less in good times, and much more in stressful, difficult periods when teamwork and synergy and reliance on each other is desperately needed. Yes, of course, there is risk of a relationship breakdown, and it might happen. But if you pre-decide rules of engagement, you minimize that possibility, and maximize the chances of emerging stronger.

Actions For You:

If your "norm" is to avoid conflict, the only way to change is to take a deep breath and simply dive in and try it. Your biggest risk is not getting the outcome you want—which is what avoidance has brought you all along anyway—so you're no worse off. And if you're worried about upsetting family or friends or co-workers, pre-empt this by first setting up rules of engagement for such discussions...rules you agree to always follow and not violate...rules that promote respect and dignity, and keep tempers at bay. Then if trouble emerges, you've got the groundwork already laid to have a civilized discussion. And the best news of all—like most things in life—the more you do it, the better you get and more comfortable you become. Before long, you'll look back on "those days when I always avoided conflict"...proud of yourself for facing it head-on and growing past it, now fearless of difficult conversations. And your decisions, your relationships, your life will be enriched.

Power Thought: "The absolute best way to become absolutely useless as a foreman, supervisor, manager, leader, parent, or friend, is to become highly skilled in the art of conflict avoidance." Greg Gilbert, author and pastor.

179

SECTION 7

Honest Conversations

How Do We Build Teamwork and Make Relationships at Work Stronger?

We take the business to new heights as a collective body. As a team, we pool our resources and collective talents. Through our team effort, we build effective processes to serve the customers. We flourish because of relationships we can collectively build. One person's weakness can be supplanted by another team member's strengths. It is said that "a rising tide raises all boats."

However, if we fail, we fail together. Our collective future is tied together. We rise and fall primarily based on our collective relationships with one another.

We spent the entire previous section on the topics of conflict and how to minimize its adverse effects on the team. This section will attempt to build on that.

Once we reduce workplace friction, it is possible to act more authentically and have more honest conversations that continue to nurture and build relationships. As relationships are strengthened, we can turn our attention to creating robust processes to better serve the customer.

It should be pointed out that skills learned in this area of authenticity and honest conversations will absolutely help with our relationships outside of the workplace as well.

This section is primarily a summary of the work of several excellent thought leaders and three amazing books:

- *Daring Greatly* by Brené Brown
- *Crucial Conversations* by Kerry Patterson and his group
- *Radical Candor* by Kim Scott

I will attempt to summarize and synthesize these books into a cohesive section on honest conversations.

Brené Brown's book, *Daring Greatly*, is a great place to start the exploration of honest conversation because she brings many words, concepts, and ideas into the discussion. Her ideas help us gain insight into the human dynamics involved in authenticity and honest conversation. Her book will act as an introduction to several important terms. These terms form a sort of common language we will use as we explore these important ideas.

Here is a basic outline of her premise.

Humans Seek to Avoid Pain

This should come as no surprise. It's one of the foundational premises of psychology that not only humans, but all animal behavior is influenced a great deal by the powerful motivation to avoid pain.

One of Brown's initial premises is that we don armor to avoid pain (psychological pain). Graphically, it looks like this:

Donning of Armor

⬆

Leads to

Pain Avoidance

This is merely saying that most humans have experienced pain of some form in their life. Those painful experiences run the gamut from being teased and made fun of as a child, to horrific abuse in all its forms. Pain is a common denominator all humans have in common. Humans, by nature, seek to avoid pain.

This pain avoidance leads to the donning of armor. Armor is a frequently used term utilized by Brown throughout her writings. She uses the word to mean "adopted ways of acting which protect us from pain."

We adopt specific ways of being and acting to protect us from further pain.

One of the tactics of donning armor is to *not* show people who we really are. As part of the armor, we might not tell people how we really feel or what we really experience. We might shut down any type of honest communication because honesty and open communication show who we really are. And if we show who we really are, we are, by definition, vulnerable. If we are vulnerable, we might get hurt and experience pain.

As we go through our lives with our armor intact, we resist communicating our needs, feelings, hopes, fears, and dreams. It should be clear to see how armor would stand as a roadblock to honesty and authenticity. In fact, an armored life is the opposite of an honest and authentic life.

Psychological armor keeps us from pain, but it also keeps us from connecting with other humans. To grow emotionally and have intimacy with other humans, it becomes necessary to remove the armor. For those who have so carefully installed the armor, this can be a challenge. The armor has been a protection, and we often are very hesitant to let down our defenses.

Now, the graphic looks like this:

Section 7: Honest Conversations

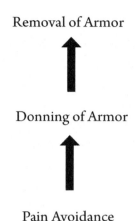

Some people are able to work hard and, over time, start the process of removing the armor. So now we have a model of human behavior that looks like this:

To have an authentic life, we must find a way to remove the armor. When we remove the armor, we have the possibility of showing who we really are. We can communicate in real terms.

In Brown's model, there is no honesty without the willingness to be vulnerable. She believes vulnerability, or the willingness to be vulnerable, is the key to an authentic/honest life.

Vulnerability is the key to open and honest conversation. When we are "armored up," to use one of Brown's terms, we cannot openly and honestly communicate. The willingness to be vulnerable opens us up to honest communication.

Graphically, it looks like this:

When we honestly and openly communicate, we have the opportunity to live authentically. That looks like this:

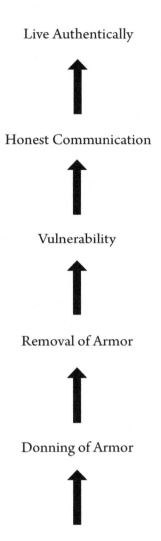

Honest and open communication allows us to move towards living authentically. Authentic living is "what you see is what you get." It is living in an open, honest way that allows others to see who you really are. Part of the willingness to be authentic is the mindset that, "however I am, I am enough." The quality of authenticity dramatically influences the way we interact with others. When we come from a place of "I am enough," we have no need (or less need) to put others down, in order to feel better about ourselves. We have less need to create cliques and groups where we feel like the "top dog." We have less need to exclude others who threaten our dominance. We are more likely to experience healthy relationships. Ultimately, authenticity allows for greater levels of internal happiness and personal joy and fulfillment. If these relationships are work-related, the workplace becomes a place for greater collaboration and innovation.

What Role Do Honesty, Authenticity, and Vulnerability Have in the Workplace?

Authenticity and vulnerability play into workplace culture in several ways. For one, team members might avoid addressing their concerns, fears, and feelings during the regular course of business life. When this happens, issues, problems, and challenges can build up and fester over time. Without honesty and authenticity, there is a distinct lack of real understanding, connection, trust, and empathy between team members. Business innovation can suffer. Innovation requires a willingness to look critically at the systems and practices of a business. As a group, we must be willing to try new methods, processes, and ultimately be willing to fail. If failure is not a part of the workplace culture, team members will not be willing to try new approaches and innovate. Team members may fear they will be blamed or punished for failure. Failure is an inherent part of innovation. Fear of failure, fear of blame, and fear of the repercussions of failure keep a lid on innovation. The result is that we stay in our comfort zone rather than venture out where it is not only uncomfortable but downright scary.

My goal over the next few pages is to explore:

- The role of honest communication in the workplace.
- How we might have *more* honest communication in our workplace.
- What role honest conversation could play in developing cohesive teams at work

186

Section 7: Honest Conversations

- When honest communication could help.
- When honest communication might cause more problems than it solves.
- What qualities team members need to cultivate to be able to have more honest conversations.

As you go through these terms, ideas, and concepts, you will start to appreciate many of the challenges that come with attempts at honest communication and authenticity in the workplace. If we tackle the hard work of honest conversation, we will need many skills for sure, but we will need to create a culture that will allow honest conversation. This section is just the beginning of the journey. This section will explore some of what we as a group will need to learn and how we can move toward more honest, authentic communication. This material is about starting the conversation and exploring the challenges inherent in real communication.

We are going to start the exploration with a series of definitions. These definitions will form a common language that will allow us to communicate these complex ideas and concepts.

Power of a Common Language

As you read through the definitions in the following pages, note how each of these terms or concepts affect the ability to have open and honest conversation. Also, note to what degree a particular topic is an issue at Oak Haven Massage and what steps we can take to address the matter in question.

Authenticity

Not false or copied. Genuine. Real. What you see is what you get.

Why is this important? We often see inauthenticity in others as a threat to our survival. This is likely because we do not trust people we deem to be inauthentic or fake.

187

Leadership: Building and Nurturing a World-Class Team of Massage Therapists

Let's explore and define the several types of conversations we might have on any given day.

Honest Conversation

An honest conversation is a conversation where you are willing to be honest, vulnerable, and seek not only to get your viewpoint across, but to also understand the other person's position. Honest conversation leads to more significant connections, greater empathy between team members, and more potential for problem-solving and business solutions. Honest conversation is characterized by honesty or the willingness to share hard things, as well as vulnerability or a willingness to reveal your actual positions.

Unfortunately, not all conversations are honest conversations.

Sometimes team members may have conversations with the wrong people. They may have conversations with people who can't answer questions or solve problems.

Categories of Honest Conversations at Work

Team member to team member. This is when we try to clear the air or solve an issue with a coworker. It's often very scary for a team member to approach a coworker with an issue or problem. It takes both courage and skill to navigate these conversations successfully. It's so much easier to talk to everyone else about the situation than directly address the issue.

Manager to a team member. This is when a team member is given feedback by their manager to help them improve their job performance. Providing feedback to team members is an art form. Every team member is different and requires a slightly different approach. We will spend a great deal of time in this section giving managers ideas about how to give feedback in the most useful way possible.

Team member to manager. Conversation initiated by the team member to make the manager aware of challenges, issues, problems, and/or concerns. This is a time to clarify, clear the air, talk about what is working

188

Section 7: Honest Conversations

and what is not working. This might be the most challenging type of conversation to have. Team members are not often given a chance to give managers feedback. Most workplace cultures do not encourage feedback "up the chain of command," to use an *Extreme Ownership* term. It can be beneficial for the manager who wants to become more effective, but it requires very specific encouragement from leaders.

Roadblocks and Challenges to Honest Conversations

Personal Behavioral Adaptations

These are adaptations each of us makes to protect ourselves and navigate the world around us. Many of these behaviors were adopted years ago and may no longer be serving us. Many of these adaptations block our ability to have open and honest communication and ultimately affect our ability to live an authentic life. At first, many of these concepts will seem simplistic, soft, touchy-feely, and undoubtedly unrelated to honesty and honest conversation in general. My hope is that as you consider these ideas, you will see the correlation between these concepts and the unwillingness to engage in honest dialogue. According to Brown, at the heart of reluctance to open up and be honest is the issue of vulnerability. In Brown's words, "I didn't set out to study vulnerability. It just happens to be the barrier to almost everything we want from our lives."

Let's start with armor, as it relates to the topic of vulnerability and open, honest conversations.

Armor

To understand and comprehend vulnerability at a deep level, we need to explore the concept of armor.

We choose various forms of armor to protect ourselves from pain. The pain we fear may be physical or emotional. It may be real or imagined. We may choose to put on armor to protect our place in the group or tribe.

Leadership: Building and Nurturing a World-Class Team of Massage Therapists

One of the greatest fears humans have is to be kicked out of the tribe. We need the safety of the tribe or group to survive. We have an intuitive sense of what will keep us in the good graces of the tribe, and we are willing to take very drastic measures to stay in good standing with the tribe. Armor may, in some situations, serve a purpose. It may serve our survival needs.

When we choose to armor up, we fear showing people around us who we really are. We are fearful of being honest with our thoughts and opinions for fear of ridicule or being ostracized. We think our honesty will affect our standing in the group.

Armor serves to protect us from attack. The definition of vulnerability is "open to attack." As we remove the armor, we are, by definition, vulnerable. Armor comes in various forms. It might involve a change in the way we think or process information. It might show up in our unwillingness to share emotions. These armoring techniques serve to shield us from emotional hurt and help us avoid pain in all its forms.

Armor has its foundation in fear. Fear that people won't accept who we really are. Fear of ridicule. Fear of ostracizing. Fear of expulsion from the group.

Armoring can show up as a lack of self-confidence or self-worth. The feeling I need to be more than I am, which means I am not enough. In our past, when others would communicate to us that we were not enough, we bought into it, so we armor up.

The armor we have may have served us at one point in our life, but it might not be serving us any longer. We often keep the armor even when it stops serving us.

> "As children, we've found ways to protect ourselves from vulnerability, from being hurt, diminished, and disappointed. We put on armor; we used our thoughts, emotions, and behaviors as weapons. And we learn how to make ourselves scarce, even disappear. As adults, we realize that to live with courage, purpose, connection, and authenticity, to be the person we long to be, we must again

Section 7: Honest Conversations

be vulnerable. We must take off the armor, put down the weapons, show up, and let ourselves be seen."

—*Dare to Lead*

Armor and Vulnerability

The dictionary defines vulnerability "capable or susceptible of being wounded or hurt."

Whenever we are honest with our feelings and impressions and show people how we really are and what we really think, we run the risk of being hurt. We can be ridiculed, made fun of, ostracized or shunned, shamed, or any number of unpleasant consequences. Our past is one predictor of what can happen when we are honest with our opinions and feelings. We might have had unpleasant experiences in the past that occurred due to our being honest about our perspectives. So, we may have learned that we do not share this kind of information.

You might choose not to be vulnerable, armor up, and never put yourself in a situation where you can be wounded or hurt. Armor protects us from hurt. Armor keeps us from showing who we really are. The thought being, "If I never show who I really am, I can never be harmed or hurt." It's our armor that keeps us unwilling to have honest conversations and to live our authentic selves. Putting armor on is the exact opposite of vulnerability and authenticity.

How Will This Information Help Me?

Everyone will do something different with this information. Some will do nothing. Some will use this information to explore the sources and impact on armor in their lives. But I want to share a critical insight and observation. Often, we don't need to actively do much to have these ideas and concepts impact our lives. You will hear me say this several times in the pages that follow. I've observed that the simple act of bringing these things

Leadership: Building and Nurturing a World-Class Team of Massage Therapists

to our awareness is often enough to start the process of internal discovery. For some, just bringing up the concept of armor is enough to kickstart the process of armor removal. This may seem counter-intuitive, but it is true. I have observed that the simple act of introducing the term "honest conversation" into our group, with no formal training, has caused a significant shift in open dialogue. So don't make this material hard or challenging to access. I'm convinced these concepts can have profound effects on us as a group by simply introducing them. Defining words and terms also create a common language to explore these ideas and share impactful insights. Vulnerability in an organization starts with the leader.

Vulnerability and Leadership

Vulnerability as a leader means being open and honest, especially regarding our weaknesses or mistakes. It's not easy to admit that you messed up or take the blame when things go wrong. As a leader, it's essential to upholding your integrity. When you make a decision, you have to own the outcome, good or bad. If you fall short on something, admit that you screwed up and apologize sincerely. People value honesty. You can't expect your team members to be accountable and transparent with you if you are not open with them.

Courage

Courage and fear are not mutually exclusive. You can feel both at the same time. Courage is the willingness to put yourself at risk for the greater good. Courage is a willingness to be vulnerable. Courage is a willingness to be misunderstood. It takes real courage to show who you really are or how you really feel. It is said that courage is feeling the fear but doing it anyway.

Curiosity

Curiosity is the quality of wanting to understand at a deeper level. Curiosity can be uncomfortable because it requires uncertainty and vulnerability.

192

Section 7: Honest Conversations

Curiosity is about listening and asking the right questions. "Tell me more" is a great curiosity tool. Curiosity and humility often go together because it takes humility to be genuinely curious. Genuine curiosity implies that you do not know everything and would like to know and understand more.

Empathy

Everywhere you turn, you hear the word empathetic. We are encouraged on all sides to be more empathetic. Let's take a minute to try to understand this term better.

Empathy is not connecting to an experience. It is connecting to the emotion that connects to the experience. We do not need firsthand experience of an event to extend empathy. We do not need to have been dumped or fired, lost a parent, sibling, or partner to relate to someone's grief. If you have ever felt grief, disappointment, shame, fear, loneliness, or anger, you're qualified to extend empathy. Empathy is not about fixing the problem or situation. Empathy is about the brave choice to be with someone in their darkness, not to race to turn on the light so we feel better. It is the connection that has a healing effect. It's not that we fix or correct the problem. Empathy is not about giving advice. It's being with someone through a difficult and challenging time. We can't take our lens off and look through someone else's, but we can honor their perspective, whatever it is. We can honor their truth, even though it's different from ours. If you're wanting to be empathetic, it's important to stay out of judgment. Let go of the fear of saying the wrong thing. Let go of the need to say the perfect thing. We do not have to be perfect at giving empathy.

On a more simplistic level, empathy might be used in the workplace to allow us to have more tolerance for our coworkers. Maybe if empathy was a little more present, we might be a bit more tolerant of our coworkers' mistakes and behaviors.

If you have the digital version of this book, click the link below for a short video by Brené Brown on empathy.

https://www.youtube.com/watch?v=1Evwgu369Jw

193

Leadership: Building and Nurturing a World-Class Team of Massage Therapists

Invisible Army

People often use "we" to express their point of view, implying that they are putting forth an opinion that is backed by invisible others. They might say, "We don't like the direction the company is headed." It's important to give your own perspectives and opinions. Pretending to represent other people's opinions is a form of criticism. It's also a form of dishonesty, and it skirts the need to exercise courage. Practice speaking for yourself, and let others do the same.

Concept of Psychological Safety

> "Simply put, psychological safety makes it possible to give tough feedback and to have difficult conversations without the need to tiptoe around the truth. In a psychologically safe environment, people believe that if they make a mistake, others will not penalize or think less of them for it. They also believe that others will not resent or humiliate them when they ask for help or information. This belief comes about when people trust and respect each other. It produces a sense of confidence that the group will not embarrass, reject, or punish someone for speaking up."
>
> —*Dare to Lead*

To have an honest and open environment, people must believe they can share their truth, and it will be okay. People must believe they can make a mistake without penalty in an environment of safety.

What gets in the way of people feeling psychologically safe?

- Judgment
- Unsolicited advice being given
- Interpreting
- Sharing outside of the group

194

Section 7: Honest Conversations

- Not interrupting
- Not keeping confidence
- Not staying curious about other perspectives, ideas, viewpoints, and opinions

Crucial Conversations

I started reading the book *Crucial Conversations* in 2012. For some reason, I only made it halfway through, then set it aside. I failed to see the brilliance in the material. After several of Oak Haven leadership sessions and our work with honest conversations, I noticed the book on my bookshelf and pulled it down. I opened the book to the foreword and noticed it was written by one of my heroes, Stephen R. Covey. I started reading and came to this:

"I encourage you to really dig into this material, to pause and think deeply about each part and how the parts are sequenced. Then apply what you've learned. Go back to the book again, learn some more, and apply your new learnings."

I was touched by this advice. I highlighted the quote, and in the margin wrote, "Vintage Covey." I decided right then to dive back into the book. It was as if Stephen Covey was giving me a little coaching session from beyond the grave. I knew I needed to roll up my sleeves and get to work, and I'm glad I did.

Here is another little pearl I found toward the end of the book:

One of the authors commented that many people had come up to him at various events and told him how much the book had helped them. His natural tendency was to ask which part. When they couldn't really tell him specifics, he tried probing with questions to understand what had been helpful.

> "As I press further, many indicate that they haven't read much of the book at all—okay, they've only scanned the book—but somehow the title, cover, headers, and first few pages have served them well. And they aren't kidding. A

quick glance has helped them enormously. How could this be? As I probe further, I learn that the simple idea—that some conversations are so important that they deserve a special title and treatment. The book served to remind individuals that they should be careful as they step up to high-stakes conversations. Instead of becoming frightened or upset and then degenerating into their worst selves, they ought to bring their best conversation skills into play. This means that readers don't have to study every concept and skill contained in this book before they risk speaking their mind. The reason I find this response so refreshing is that it offers so much hope. You don't have to read every syllable contained in this book, go into intense training for months, and then emerge with the minimum skill set to survive a crucial conversation."

I've also noticed that very rudimentary skills with this material can yield incredible results. I'm convinced that we can all improve our results with important conversations with even one or two fundamental elements of understanding that we can put into practice. Of course, the more skills we master, the better, but even a modest effort with these concepts will help us immensely.

Crucial conversations are interactions that happen every day that affect your life. They are the regular day-to-day conversations you have with regular people, not kings, presidents, or emperors. They have three components:

1. Stakes are high
2. Opinions vary
3. Emotions run strong

Section 7: Honest Conversations

What makes some conversations crucial, and not just challenging, frustrating, frightening, or annoying, is that the results of the conversation could have a significant impact on the quality of your life. Some discussions have the potential to alter your daily routine forever.

There are three options for crucial conversations:

1. Avoid them
2. Face them and handle them poorly
3. Face them and handle them well

One hallmark of a crucial conversation is that our first reaction is to avoid it if possible. The following are four basic premises of the crucial conversation's framework.

Basic Premise #1

When Conversations Matter Most, We Are Often on Our Worst Behavior

Why? Because we go into survival mode. Adrenaline goes into the bloodstream, and we go into a fight or flight mode, which shunts blood from our brain to our muscles. This concept is useful because once we realize that our adrenalin can hijack an important conversation, we can watch for this, and take steps to lessen its destructive impact.

Basic Premise #2

The Power of Useful Dialogue

Useful dialogue is the free flow of information, feelings, and opinions between people. If we continue to speak respectfully, seeking to understand the other person's viewpoint, we will often make progress. Useful dialogue includes concepts such as safety, trust, respect, curiosity, and seeking mutual goals. Before you can pursue mutual goals, you must know what the other's goals are. The purpose of dialogue is to create a shared

Leadership: Building and Nurturing a World-Class Team of Massage Therapists

pool of information and meaning, as opposed to a personal pool of information and meaning. The goal is to have each person contribute to this shared pool. The authors of *Crucial Conversations* are continually talking about the "shared pool of knowledge and information." Their viewpoint is that this is a key component to successful communication. Having a shared pool of knowledge versus our own individual pools of knowledge. The idea being that if we are drawing from a common pool of knowledge, we will be a step closer to understanding each other.

The alternative to "staying in dialogue" is to withhold information and meaning by two behaviors: The first is **silence**. We may feel that withholding information serves us in some way. It usually does not. The second is **personal verbal attack**. Someone might attack our character, our motives, or our intelligence.

Both of these are a form of using manipulation to get our way. The authors refer to these two behaviors as silence and violence.

Basic premise #3
Don't Limit Your Choices (aka Fool's Choice)

Sometimes we adopt the belief that we have to choose between two harmful alternatives. For example, we think we have to stay silent or we have to offend someone. In reality, these are not our only two choices. Between these two polar opposites are an infinite number of better options. It is wise for us to remember this. **This premise is one of the most useful and important concepts I took from my reading of this book.**

Basic Premise #4
Create safety

The opposite of safety is fear. Fear creates defensiveness. We might fear being attacked or humiliated. The concept here is to make it safe for people. People are always watching out for unsafe situations. People will contribute to the shared pool of knowledge and meaning as long as they feel safe. To encourage the other person to stay in dialogue and contribute to the shared pool of meaning, it is useful to carefully observe others. Watch when safety is at risk for others or when someone appears fearful.

Whenever you notice you have gone "out of dialogue," look for safety issues. When people don't feel safe, they go into fear and resort to silence or violence (verbal abuse) as protection, becoming defensive because they feel unsafe. This is so simple and yet profound, and it's a fundamental principle of their book.

When we are verbally attacked, our natural tendency is to attack back. That only reinforces the safety issues felt. "See, I was right, they are attacking me." In this way, feelings of a lack of safety is a self-fulfilling prophecy.

If we can re-frame the silence or the attack as an indicator they feel unsafe, we can do something to help them feel safe. When you recognize safety issues, stay curious, and try to avoid getting angry or frightened, try to restore safety rather than react negatively.

Silence can take the form of avoiding or withdrawal. **Violence** can take the form of controlling, labeling, or attacking. It's useful to continually ask ourselves, "How do I make it safe for those who feel threatened?"

How Do You Make It Safe?

The first condition of safety is a **mutual purpose**. Try to find something you both want and work toward that goal. Find an area where you both can work toward a mutually beneficial outcome. Is there a shared goal, interest, or purpose you can both focus on? Mutual purpose can serve as an entry point to dialogue. It is important to understand that mutual purpose is not a technique. You must sincerely care and be worthy of trust. Once you find a shared goal or purpose, it is vital to communicate your commitment to the shared goal.

The second condition of safety is **mutual respect**. In every aspect of your interaction, you must be worthy of trust and respect. Likewise, it is important to show trust and respect to those you are in dialogue with.

Respect is like air—as long as it's present, no one thinks about it. But take it away, and it's all you can think about. Sometimes people make it challenging to have a feeling of respect. What do you do in situations when respect is difficult to feel? One thing you can do is look for aspects of their basic humanity that you can respect. Maybe they are a father or mother. Perhaps they have some element of their behavior you can focus on. Find some way to feel a sense of respect towards them.

If you see silence, violence, attacking, aggressive behavior, or sarcasm in the other person, see these as a sign of a lack of safety, and move to build security. Step out of the conversation, build safety. You can do this by reviewing your mutual purpose: "It seems like we are both trying to force our views on each other. I commit to stay in this discussion until we have a solution that satisfies us both." You can apologize, if necessary, then step back in.

When conversations turn critical, we are not our best due to the chemistry of emotions. The skills to be effective in critical conversations are learnable and will make a difference. Ask, What do I really want here, for myself, for others, for the relationship? Clarify what you really want. Clarify what you really do not want. Always start with a mutual purpose, something you both want and can get behind. Mutual purpose and mutual respect are essential components in creating a safe environment where real, honest communication can occur.

Master Our Stories

Creating Stories and Attaching Meaning

Humans love stories. Stories help us make sense of the world. When we see actions by other people, we look for ways to explain that behavior, often creating a story about the behavior we see. Our mind is continually looking at the events around us, then interpreting the events in an attempt to understand.

For example, let's take a situation where a coworker is on her phone while you are doing many office chores that both of you are supposed to be working on.

Section 7: Honest Conversations

You become upset because she is not helping. Let's say you managed to get through your shift without confronting her. The following day, you told a different coworker that she was lazy and not a good work-mate. As it usually does, your conversation got back to the original coworker, the one who was not helping, and a whole lot of office drama followed.

Let's break this scenario down.

The initial fact of this situation is that your coworker did not help with the office chores. This is true. You will likely make up a story in your mind about why your coworker didn't help. You assign a meaning to the behavior you have observed. You will often assign the meaning based on what you think are extremely valid reasons. Most of us are really good at this. So good that we believe the meaning we assign to a particular behavior is accurate. We forget that we really don't know why people do what they do or say what they say. We forget that we made up a story about their behavior to help us make sense of the situation.

If you can think of a situation like this from your own life, you are not alone. All humans attach meaning to events to weave together a story. Some parts of the story are factual; you have firsthand knowledge. Much of the story is manufactured by your brain. We fill in the details that are missing. And guess what is nearly always missing? The reasons people do what they do. We rarely know this. We have to fill in that part of the story with our imagination. And then we take action based on the story we have manufactured.

It's a protective mechanism that we developed over hundreds of thousands of years. It was formed as a protection to us when our ancestors lived on the savannah in Africa. Our ancestor's survival depended on their ability to quickly attach meaning to events. They might be exposed to an event, like a lion's roar, and immediately attach meaning to it. They would hear the roar and immediately think of danger. They would also have an immediate emotional response, such as fear that led to quick action, such as running away.

201

It might be diagramed something like this:

This phenomenon of attaching meaning was fine-tuned concerning human interactions as well. When we came into contact with a neighboring group of humans, we had to quickly size up the situation. We would need to attach meaning to anything that the visiting humans would do. Did they mean us harm? We had to pick up on subtle cues. If we didn't, we might not survive the visit.

When the visiting human raised his hand, was he making a peace sign, or was he raising a spear? Our ability to attach meaning to events has served us well for a long time. But because it needs to happen fast, we are often wrong about the meaning. Another interesting note is when we attach meaning to an event, it often serves us well to assume the event is a threat. So, over the years, our ancestors developed a bias for negativity. In the early days of

Section 7: Honest Conversations

human development, if we came across a group of humans, and one raised his arm, we would run or fight. Our bias for negativity would cause us to defend ourselves. It was better for our survival that when the visitor raised his arm, we protect ourselves rather than give him the benefit of the doubt and end up with a spear in us.

This same mechanism is going on within our minds today. We continuously evaluate the events around us.

These events fall into two main categories:

1.   Actions by others
2.   Words spoken by those around us

We are continually evaluating and attaching meaning to the actions and words of others. This is yet another way of saying we are constantly attaching meaning to events. These meanings we attach are made up; **they are stories we are telling ourselves**. Sometimes these stories are accurate; often, they are not. We didn't know what our coworker meant when she said, "Nice tie," so we arbitrarily assigned meaning; we make up something, such as, *She hates my tie.*"

Remember, as a protection, we have a bias towards a negative meaning. The meaning we attach causes us to have an emotional response. Our emotional response can have a wide range of possibilities; fear is just one of the options. It could be anger, embarrassment, frustration, or a host of other emotions. We don't always attach a negative meaning. Sometimes we err on the positive side...but this is rare. It goes back to our genetic bias. Being negative helps keep us safer.

Now that you have a bit of a background into this phenomenon, we are ready to tackle the issue of your coworker not helping you with the office chores.

As you will recall, she was on her phone and not helping. This caused you to feel upset. It's important to point out you are not upset because she didn't help you. You're upset because of the meaning you have attached

203

Leadership: Building and Nurturing a World-Class Team of Massage Therapists

to her not helping. This is a critical distinction. It is rarely the event that upsets us. It's the meaning we attach to the event. You were convinced that she is mad at you because you didn't give her that last donut this morning. So, she is being petty and refusing to help—at least that is the story you have made up in your mind. You have observed an event, she didn't help you. No arguing this point, events are objective, it really happened. It is the meaning we attach to the event that is made up. We think it is real because it happens so fast, and we have lots of reasons and a solid rationale about what the event means.

And now, the more you think about her pettiness, the madder you get. You eventually devise a plan. You will show her. That's it, the perfect retaliation, you will give her the silent treatment. So, you don't say a word to her for the next two hours of your shift.

We have all been on one side or the other of this type of situation.

One of the cures for the harmful effects of assigning negative meanings to events is simply to *realize* that you are assigning meaning. Realize that you just made a story up. You don't know why they did what they did. If we backtracked on this example, you don't really know why your coworker is not helping with the chores. You made some assumptions, but you really don't know for sure. The power of this insight is that, once you work with this concept for a while, you start to catch yourself attaching meaning to events (making up stories). If you can catch yourself attaching meaning, you can change the meaning you attach. This skill will change your life. It is well worth giving thought to this phenomenon. I encourage you to practice the fine art of attaching meaning. Practice creating meaning that creates a positive emotion in you versus a negative emotion.

I've worked with this concept for many years. I have indeed become better and better at catching myself in the act of making up something that is negative. But, if I was really truthful, it's more often my daughters these days who catch me making up stories. They will hear

204

Section 7: Honest Conversations

me say something about a situation and say, "Well, you really don't know, you've attached a meaning. It might actually be something else." I can't begin to count the number of times they have caught me attaching a negative meaning to a situation and called me out on it. It gives them great pleasure to do this because guess how they learned this? Throughout their entire lives, I would point out to them when they had attached a negative meaning to an event. I would use the experience as a teaching moment and show them how they might re-think the situation and attach a different meaning. I would encourage them to attach a meaning that would be a little less emotionally charged. Now that they are adults, they delight in pointing out when I'm doing what I always taught them *not* to do. These experiences with my daughters have taught me that it's often easier to see this dynamic play out with others than to catch ourselves in the act.

This example above illustrates three concepts that contribute to workplace conflict:

- Attaching meaning to events or something we observe.
- Creating a negative story about what we observe.
- Assuming we understand the motivations behind a particular behavior.

It's often not the behavior that bothers us…it's the motive behind the action that we think we understand that causes us frustration.

Path to Action

In *Crucial Conversations*, Kerry Patterson and his group go over a variation of the material above. They refer to it as "managing your stories" or the "path to action." Both of these descriptions are useful. We humans are always making up stories, so it is helpful to manage them. There is a path or sequence of events that we routinely follow as we make the stories up. Let's take a minute to go over their **path to action** concept. It's very similar to the steps I outlined above, with some slight variations.

Below is a graphic of the path to action.

Critical Conversion, 'Path to Action'
p. 109
book

We see or hear something. We tell ourselves a story about what we saw or heard. This story causes us to feel a certain way (creates an internal state). This internal state often leads us to act or take action. Hence the term **path to action**.

I have found this model of how humans interpret events and create stories to explain those events some of the most useful information I have ever learned. Let me give you some examples of how this model can unfold.

Section 7: Honest Conversations

It starts out with an event (something you see or hear). For example, let's say you call your sister and you leave a message. Then, after one week, she does not call you back. This is an event.

Next, you interpret the event or ask yourself what this means. You make up a story.

Depending on what story you make up, you will feel a certain way. If you tell yourself she did not return your call because she was busy, that causes one set of feelings. If you tell yourself, *She doesn't care about me,* that creates a different set of emotions.

Let's explore this in another way. The event is objective; it really happened. Your sister did not return your phone call. No one would or could dispute this. The interpretation or the story we make up is fabricated(-subjective). It's not real. The problem is, we often forget or fail to realize that it's something we made up. We think the story we tell ourselves is real. That is why the topic here is **managing your stories**. If we are thoughtful, we can create stories that empower us rather than disempower us. If we practice, we can create stories that cause us to feel good, rather than angry or upset.

Ten people can have the same objective event happen (such as my sister did not return my phone call). All ten people can have completely different interpretations of the event. We all interpret the world around us differently because we all have different experiences, values, backgrounds, and education. Each of us sees the world through our own lens; it's like each of us has our own unique pair of glasses through which we view the world. Another way to look at this is that we filter every event that happens to us through our own unique filter. I call this filter the meta filter because it is all-encompassing.

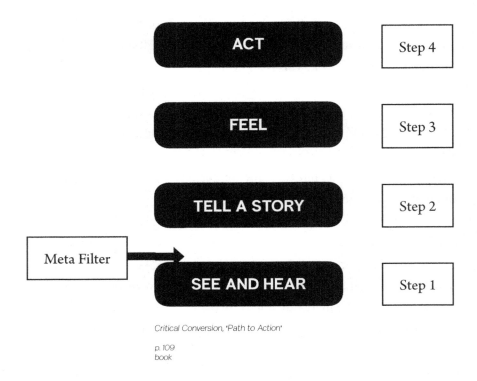

Critical Conversion, "Path to Action"

p. 109
book

Another way to describe step two (above) is to say we all interpret events differently based on our lens or filter. When we interpret, we attach meaning to the event. This is something we all do. We are hard-wired to ask ourselves, *What does this mean?* We cannot help it. Interpretation is often described as **creating a story** or attaching meaning. We create a story (interpretation) about what just happened. We do it unconsciously. We do it continually. We do it fast. And we all do it differently depending on our lens or filters. The event is objective—it really happened. The interpretation is subjective—it's something we made up. We think it is true, but it's most likely just a story.

Section 7: Honest Conversations

Depending on what story we tell about what just happened, we feel a particular emotion or feeling, such as happy, sad, frustrated, or mad. It's possible to feel any one of dozens of emotions.

Let's recap where we are so far.

Step 1. There is an event. Events are subjective—they really happened.

Step 2. We interpret the event through our own unique filter or lens. Part of the interpretation process is creating a story—we assign meaning to the event to help explain the event. This is subjective. Ten people could experience the same event and tell ten different stories based on their unique lens or filters.

Step 3. We experience an emotion based on the story we just told ourselves. It could be happiness, sadness, or anger.

Step 4. We take action based on how we feel. If we are angry, we act one way; if we are sad, we act another way. It is important to note that the above sequence happens very, very fast. It has been honed over eons as a protection to us. It is built in to our physiology, just like we do not have to think when we touch something hot. We pull our hand away as a reflex. It is the same with this four-step pathway; it all happens in a nanosecond. So fast that we have no time to give it rational thought. We just accept it as fact. We fail to realize that we just make up a story.

Understanding this sequence is extraordinarily powerful. The critical point being, it's the story or interpretation that causes us to feel a certain way, not the actual event itself. Because this interpretation or story is made up, we can choose to make up or create a different meaning to any event that comes within our awareness. This isn't necessarily easy, but it is possible to catch ourselves creating a story. When we do this, we can go back to the event and create a new story—*My sister isn't disrespecting me; she's just busy.* We do have control of our stories.

The authors of *Crucial Conversations* call this sequence the **path to action**. The authors point out that under normal circumstances, our stories control us. Our stories first control how we feel. Then our story controls how we act.

In the book, the authors have a full section entitled *Master My Stories* that explains this model. It encourages the readers to understand this process and take control of their stories.

How Do We Control Our Stories?

We can control our stories by working backward from the emotion (Step 3). The key here is awareness. We can practice being aware of the emotions we are feeling and what leads to the emotion.

We are angry because Bill made a rude comment about my tie. But wait, I interpreted this; I made that story up. I can make up a new story that doesn't cause me to be angry.

We can start taking control of our stories by being aware of the emotions we are feeling. We can work backward to the interpretation and the event. The authors call this "getting back to the facts." Getting back to the facts means we focus on what was objective. That which cannot be disputed. That which occurred before we made the interpretation or created the story. If we get back to the facts, we can attach a more useful and less charged meaning and move back through the process or path. This takes practice, but it really does change the way we feel about the events we experience.

Watch for Clever Stories

Watch for and be aware of three specific categories of stories we tell ourselves. The authors refer to these as **clever stories**.

- **Victim stories.** Victim stories are stories we tell ourselves about how we are the victim. The other person is bad, wrong, or dumb. We are good, right, or brilliant. When we tell a victim story, we ignore the role we played in the issue or problem. We can re-tell

Section 7: Honest Conversations

the story by asking what role we played in the situation and noticing how selective our perception has been.

- **Villain stories.** Villain stories are created by turning normal, decent human beings into villains. In victim stories, we exaggerate our own innocence. In villain stories, we overemphasize the other person's guilt or stupidity.

- **Helpless stories.** In helpless stories, we make up a story in which we are powerless or at the mercy of someone or some force. To get ourselves out of a helpless story, we can work to relax our absolute certainty long enough to consider other possible stories.

Both victim stories and villain stories are unfair caricatures of others. Both often involve us claiming to know the intentions or motives of others. We can move past villain stories by asking ourselves, *Why would a reasonable, rational, and decent person do what they are doing?* We can try to turn villains into humans.

What Do We Do With Our Stories?

Now that we understand how and why we create stories, we are able to consider what we can do when we realize we have created a story. When we are in a crucial conversation, the best thing we can do with our stories is share them. Let others know what you are thinking and invite them to help you gain clarity...and ask others to do the same. This increases the shared pool of knowledge and information.

The authors recommend that you start with the facts, the objective portion of the path. Share what you have observed. Then share the story you have created based on the observation. So, they are really saying you should share your path, not just the story.

211

Critical Conversion, "Path to Action"
p. 109
book

Here are several key concepts to approach a crucial conversation when considering sharing your path.

Honesty

The first is honest clarity. Honesty is about the commitment to speak to the right person and communicate the message with clarity. This is easier said than done. One of the main issues here is to make sure we are speaking to the right person. If Sara has a problem with Ashley at work, Sara's husband, friends, and coworkers may know about the issue. Sara has likely spoken about the issue to everyone but Ashley. To solve the problem, Sara must be honest with Ashley.

Section 7: Honest Conversations

Humility

Humility can be defined in many ways. Here, humility is knowing there are different lenses through which people see the world; ours is not the only one. Approach the conversation with this in mind. Humility is going into the conversation knowing we are operating out of our story and that it is just that, a story that we have told ourselves. Humility is understanding the facts are different than the story. Humility is going into a conversation looking for more information and being willing to change your mind as more information comes forward. Humility means seeking to add meaning and information to the shared pool of knowledge. Humility is going into a conversation with a win-win attitude.

Curiosity

Seek to understand the other position before seeking to be understood.

Tell your story when the time is right, but present it as a story, not the truth. The truth here is the facts, not the story.

An Example of Creating a Story

Here is an example of a conversation between Bob and his wife Carole from the *Crucial Conversations* book.

> Bob has just walked in the door, and his wife, Carole, looks upset. He can tell from her swollen eyes that she's been crying. Only when he walks in the door, Carole doesn't turn to him for comfort. Instead, she looks at him with an expression that says, "How could you?" Bob doesn't know it yet, but Carole thinks he's having an affair. He's not.
>
> How did Carole come to this dangerous and wrong conclusion? Earlier that day, she had been going over the credit card statement when she noticed a charge from the Good Night Motel. This motel was a cheap place located not more than a mile from their home.

213

Leadership: Building and Nurturing a World-Class Team of Massage Therapists

Why would he stay in a motel so close to home? she wonders. *And why didn't I know about it?* Then it hits her—*That unfaithful jerk!*

Now, what's the worst way Carole might handle this? What's the worst way of bringing the topic up to Bob? Most people agree that jumping in with an ugly accusation followed by a threat is a good candidate for that distinction. It is also what most people do, and Carole is no exception.

"I can't believe you're doing this to me," she says in a painful tone. "Doing what?" Bob asks, not knowing what she's talking about, but figuring that whatever it is, it can't be good. "You know what I'm talking about," she says, continuing to keep Bob on edge. *Do I need to apologize for missing her birthday?* Bob wonders to himself. "I'm sorry, I don't know what you're talking about," he responds, taken aback. "You're having an affair, and I have the proof right here!" Carole explains, holding up a piece of crumpled paper. "What's on that paper that says I'm having an affair?" he asks. Bob is completely befuddled because (1) he's not having an affair, and (2) the paper contains not a single compromising photo. "It's a motel bill, you jerk. You take some woman to a motel, and you put it on the credit card?! I can't believe you're doing this to me!"

Now, if Carole were sure that Bob was having an affair, perhaps this kind of talk would be warranted. It may not be the best way to work through the issue, but Bob would at least understand why Carole made the accusations and hurled threats. But, in truth, she only has a piece of paper with some numbers on it. This tangible piece of evidence has made her suspicious. How should she talk about this nasty hunch in a way that leads to dialogue?

What did Carole do wrong in this crucial conversation? She started with her story. She assumed the story was fact. She started with accusations. In doing this, she destroyed safety, and she put Bob on the defensive.

It turns out that Bob had lunch at a restaurant owned by the same people who owned the motel. When the credit card was used to pay the lunch

Section 7: Honest Conversations

bill, the card was processed through the wrong merchant account. It was an internal error.

Where Should She Have Started?

A good place to start would have been coming from a place of humility (see above). She could have also started with the facts, not her story. When possible, always start with the facts. Facts are the least controversial. Facts are the most persuasive. Facts are the least insulting. If you start with your story and kill safety, you may never get to the facts. Then bring in the story as a story, not as the truth.

Why Bring in the Story at All?

You bring in the story because the facts alone are rarely worth mentioning; it's the story that came after the facts that is cause for the emotional upheaval. Carole should have said, "These are the facts. This is the story I'm telling myself. Help me understand what is really going on."

She could have gone in with curiosity, seeking to understand, and engaging in listening. There will be plenty of time for screaming if the situation warrants it later. For now, stay in dialogue.

After sharing your facts and story, ask for the other person's view. Remember, they have facts and stories too. This allows the pool of meaning and information to expand.

Talk Tentatively

Talk tentatively—meaning, unsure or uncertain, not definite.
   Examples:

- "Perhaps you were not aware…"
- "In my opinion…"
- "I'm beginning to wonder…"
- "The story I'm telling myself is…"

215

Leadership: Building and Nurturing a World-Class Team of Massage Therapists

Speaking tentatively is the opposite of speaking in absolutes. The more tentatively you speak, the more people are open to your opinions. The authors are careful to point out that tentative is not wimpy. After sharing your story, invite the other person to help you understand when you might be wrong. It is important that you ask for opposing views. When you invite opposing views, you must mean it. You must have your heart right and want to hear from them. Encourage them with sincerity to share with you any areas of incomplete knowledge you have. Encourage this. Be curious and be patient. Seek to increase the shared pool of knowledge.

A Key Insight About Other People's Stories

When others are upset and start to tell us their story, we are getting in at the end of the process, even though it may be very early on in the conversation. Remember:

Event → interpretation or story →
feeling or emotion → action

This process may well have reached the action stage by the time we hear about their story. They may have reached the action stage where they are accusing, angry, taking cheap shots. If we respond in kind, the conversation could turn nasty in a hurry. In situations like this, we rarely think, *My, what an interesting story he must be telling himself. I wonder what led to that story.*

We often respond with our own anger, accusations, and cheap shots, and the conversation goes badly.

The Authors Had an Excellent Example in the Book

They described a situation where you were looking forward to watching a mystery movie. The movie was following a football game. The football game ran into overtime. By the time the station switched over to the movie, the message at the bottom of the screen said, *We join this program already in progress.* It is fifteen minutes into the movie. The foundation of the mystery has already been laid. You have a hard time following the movie's plotline since you do not have the starting foundational plot points.

How do you get others to share their stories?

Ask—invite them to tell you their story. Common invitations include:

- "What's going on?"
- "I'd love to hear your opinion on this."
- "Please let me know if you see it differently."
- "Don't worry about hurting my feelings—I really want to hear your thoughts on this."

Don't push too hard. Remember, we are trying to understand another's point of view, not necessarily agree with it or support it. Understanding does not equate agreement.

Most arguments are battles over 5-10 percent of the issues. We often forget that we are in agreement with 90-95 percent of the issues. Start with the 90-95 percent of the facts or story that you agree on. If you agree with aspects of the other person's story, say so and move on. Don't turn an agreement into an argument. Once you have agreed on the common ground, you can state the areas you disagree on. But express them as a difference in stories, in viewpoints. You are not saying they are wrong. You are saying the two of you are seeing things differently. You could say, "I think we are seeing things differently. Let me try to describe how…"

Final Thoughts from the Authors

"For some readers, a simple reminder that they have moved from a casual discussion to a crucial conversation helps them to be on their best behavior. Of course, learning and applying more communication skills better prepares one to deal with a variety of situations. However, if you want to get started with crucial conversations, grab but one idea from this book and bring it into your

Leadership: Building and Nurturing a World-Class Team of Massage Therapists

next high-stakes interaction. It may be just what you need to find a way to speak your mind and make it safe for others to do the same."

"If you do everything we tell you to do in this book, exactly the way we tell you to do it, and the other person doesn't want to dialogue, dialogue will not take place."

The book's title is *Crucial Conversations*—conversations is plural, meaning many, not one. The temptation is to think of a crucial conversation as your one chance to solve this problem, or the one conversation needed to save a relationship, or the one opportunity to make everything right. It may take several different conversations before you find a resolution.

Radical Candor

Kim Scott's *Radical Candor* is a mixture of Scott's ideas and Steven's commentary. I encourage you to purchase and read this excellent book.

It serves as a bridge between the "softer" concepts of vulnerability and honest conversations, to the more practical ideas of the day-to-day management of people. You will use all the concepts and principles outlined thus far as you venture into the ideas of *Radical Candor*. Scott has a very clear way of helping us see the benefits and usefulness of straight forward honesty. She also does an admirable job of describing the management pitfalls of a lack of directness or, as she calls it, a lack of candor. I love the way she takes real-world examples of honesty and frankness and explains the effects of both at work.

Three Dimensions of Radical Candor

Scott starts her book by outlining the "Three Dimensions of Radical Candor." The **first dimension** is to **care personally** about the people you lead. To care personally is about being more than just professional. It's about **giving a damn**. It's about sharing more than just your work self. It's about encouraging everyone who reports to you to care as well. It's not enough to care

Section 7: Honest Conversations

only about people's ability to perform a job. To have a good relationship, you have to be your whole self and care about each person who works for you as a human being. It's not just business; it is personal, deeply personal. Part of why people fail to care personally is the injunction to keep it professional. In addition to the obsessive devotion to professionalism, there's another, less virtuous reason why people fail to care personally. When they become a boss, some people consciously or unconsciously begin to feel they're better or smarter than those who work for them.

Caring personally is the antidote to both robotic professionalism and managerial arrogance. This idea about really caring about the people you lead is a core concept in *Radicle Candor*, and it Scott's philosophy. We must care enough about those we are called to lead to give them our accurate, honest feedback. When we choose to give honest feedback, we are being courageous and vulnerable. We are taking a risk that we will offend the person we lead. Scott's position is that leaders must be willing to take these risks. That is what leaders are paid to do.

Hopefully, you can see why I started this section on honest communication with Brené Brown's thoughts on vulnerability. The ability to be vulnerable is a key component in a manager's effectiveness.

The **second dimension** is **honest communication.** This means telling people when their work isn't good enough—and when it is; It means being honest when they are not going to get that new position they wanted. It means being forthright when you're going to hire a new boss "over" them. We may have to pull the plug on people occasionally. There are times when the results don't justify further investment in what they're working on, and we have to tell them. Delivering hard feedback is an integral part of good management.

Managers must make hard calls about who does what on a team and hold a high bar for results. Aren't these the job duties of any manager? Scott thinks so, but most managers struggle with doing these things.

The **third dimension** is **challenge directly.**

219

Leadership: Building and Nurturing a World-Class Team of Massage Therapists

"**Radical candor**" is what happens when you put **Care Personally**, **Communicate Honestly** and **Challenge Directly** together. Radical Candor builds trust and opens the door for the kind of communication that helps you achieve the results you are aiming for. And it directly addresses the fears people express when they ask questions about the management dilemmas they face. It turns out that when people trust you and believe you care about them, they are much more likely to:

- Accept and act on your praise and criticism.
- Tell you what they really think about what you are doing well and, more importantly, not doing so well.
- Engage in this same behavior with one another.
- Embrace their role on the team.
- Focus on getting results.

Why Radical?

Scott says she chose this word because so many are conditioned to avoid saying what we really think. This is partially adaptive social behavior; it helps us avoid conflict or embarrassment. But in a boss, that kind of avoidance is disastrous. Former Secretary of State Colin Powell once remarked, "Being responsible sometimes means pissing people off."

You have to accept that sometimes people on your team will be mad at you. In fact, if nobody is ever mad at you, you probably aren't challenging your team enough.

Being too "Nice."

Here's a paradox of being a good boss. Most people prefer the challenging "jerk" to the boss whose niceness gets in the way of candor. There's an article that claimed most people would rather work for a "competent asshole" than a "nice incompetent." Of course, no one wants to be incompetent. Nor do they want to be an asshole. Fortunately, the "asshole

220

Section 7: Honest Conversations

or incompetent" thing is a false dichotomy: you don't have to choose between those two extremes.

Wanting People to Like You

Apple's Chief Design Officer Jony Ive told a story about when he pulled his punches when criticizing his team's work. When Steve Jobs asked Jony why he hadn't been clearer about what was wrong, Jony replied, "Because I care about the team." To which Steve replied, "No, Jony, you're just really vain. You just want people to like you." Recounting the story, Jony said, "I was terribly upset because I knew he was right." That's why Colin Powell said leadership is sometimes about being willing to piss people off.

Give a damn about the people you challenge. But don't worry so much if they give a damn about you. Worrying about if they like you is counterproductive. That apprehension will not help your team achieve excellent results or take a step in the direction of their dreams. Let go of vanity and care personally.

Why Candor?

The key to getting everyone used to being direct when challenging each other (and you!) is emphasizing that it's necessary to communicate clearly and honestly enough so that there's no room for interpretation. Implicit with candor is that you are simply offering your perspective and viewpoint as to what is going on in a given situation.

It's Your Job to Be Critical

From the moment you learned to speak, you started to challenge those around you. Then you were told some version of, "If you don't have anything nice to say, don't say anything at all." Well, now it's your job to say it. And if you are a boss or a person in a position of some authority, it's not just your job. It's your moral obligation. Just say it!

221

Leadership: Building and Nurturing a World-Class Team of Massage Therapists

What Radical Candor is Not

Radical candor is not a license to be overly harsh or to "front-stab." It's not radical candor just because you begin with the words, "Let me be radically candid with you." If you follow that phrase with words like, "You are a liar and I don't trust you," or, "You're a dipshit," you've just acted like a garden-variety jerk. It's not radical candor if you don't show that you care personally. Radical Candor is also not an invitation to nitpick. Challenging people directly takes real energy—not only from the people you're challenging but from you as well. So, do it only for things that really matter. A good rule of thumb for any relationship is to **leave three unimportant things unsaid each day**.

Radical candor is not a hierarchical thing. To be radically candid, you need to practice it up the chain of command, down the chain of command, and sideways.

It's Not Mean; It's Clear!

Radical candor doesn't just occur at work. Every so often, a stranger offers some radical candor, and it can change your life if you're listening. This happened to me (Kim) shortly after I adopted a golden retriever puppy named Belvedere. I adored Belvedere and spoiled her. As a result, she was completely out of control. One evening, we were out for a walk, and Belvy began to tug at her leash as we waited at a crosswalk, even though cars were speeding by only a few feet in front of us. "Come on, sweetie, sit," I implored. "The light will be green in a second." Despite my reassurances, she yanked even harder on the leash and tried to lunge into the street. A stranger also waiting to cross looked over at me and said, "I can see you really love your dog." In the two seconds it took him to say those words, he established that he cared and that he wasn't judging me. Next, he gave me a challenge. "But that dog will die if you don't teach her to sit!" Direct, almost breathtakingly so. Then, without asking for permission, the man

Section 7: Honest Conversations

bent down to Belvy, pointed his finger at the sidewalk, and said with a loud, firm voice, "SIT!"

She sat. I gaped in amazement. He smiled and explained, "**It's not mean. It's clear!**" The light changed, and he strode off, leaving me with words to live by.

I hope I've never spoken to a person like a dog, but I'll never forget the stranger's words. "It's not mean, it's clear!" has become a management mantra, helping me become a better manager.

Radical Candor Starts with You...the Boss

Often when I talk to people about developing a culture of radical candor, they agree with the idea but feel nervous about putting it into practice. My advice is to explain the concept and then ask people to be radically candid with you. Start by **getting** feedback, in other words, not by dishing it out. You can do this by inviting team members to challenge you. Start by asking for criticism, not by giving it. Don't dish it out before you show you can take it. There are several reasons why it makes sense to begin building a culture of radical candor by asking people to criticize you. First, it's the best way to show you are aware you are often wrong and that you want to hear about it when you are; you want to be challenged. Second, you'll learn a lot—few people scrutinize you as closely as do those who report to you. Third, the more firsthand experience you have with how it feels to receive criticism, the better idea you'll have of how your own guidance lands for others. Fourth, asking for criticism is a great way to build trust and strengthen your relationships. Bosses get radically candid guidance from their teams not merely by being open to criticism but by actively soliciting it. **If a person is bold enough to criticize you, do not critique their criticism**. If you see somebody criticizing a peer inappropriately, say something. But if somebody criticizes you inappropriately, your job is to listen with the intent to understand and then to reward the candor. The hardest part of building this trust is asking people to challenge you just as

223

Leadership: Building and Nurturing a World-Class Team of Massage Therapists

directly as you are challenging them. When you do start giving feedback, start with praise, not criticism. When you move on to criticism, make sure you understand where the dangerous border between radical candor and obnoxious aggression is.

Encourage Feedback in Your 1-on-1

To help team members be willing to give feedback, I adopted a go-to question that Fred Kofman, author of *Conscious Business*, suggested: "What could I do or stop doing that would make it easier to work with me?" If those words don't fall easily off your tongue, find words that do. Of course, you're not really just looking for one thing; that opening question is only designed to get things moving.

Listen with the Intent to Understand, Not to Respond

You've finally gotten the other person to offer some criticism. Once again, you have to manage your response. *Whatever you do, don't start criticizing the criticism.* Don't try to explain away the comment. Instead, try to repeat what the person said to make sure you've understood it, rather than defending yourself against the criticism you've just heard. Listen to and clarify the criticism—but don't debate it. Try saying, "So what I hear you saying is…" or some variation of this language.

In some cases, of course, you may disagree with the criticism. It's here that your feedback skills become essential. It is never enough to simply acknowledge the other person's feelings. Instead, first, find something in the criticism you can agree with to signal that you're open to criticism. Then check for understanding—repeat what you heard back to the person to make sure you got it.

Getting Feedback from Your Team

Getting accurate, honest feedback from people is an art form. I wish it was as easy as simply asking someone for feedback. In general, people are

224

Section 7: Honest Conversations

delighted to give you feedback, as long as it's positive feedback. Everyone enjoys being nice and sharing good news. People by nature are very hesitant to provide you with bad news. Yet, receiving feedback, all feedback, especially negative feedback, is critical for your development as a manager.

Why is getting accurate feedback so difficult? It has to do with the way humans are wired.

We are tribal by nature—human beings developed over millions of years to get along with other humans. We are cautious to not upset other humans. We discovered long ago that upsetting other humans could be hazardous to our health.

We intuitively understand that giving someone bad news, in the form of negative feedback, can upset the person who hears the negative feedback.

So, in general, we are very careful to not rock the boat and give people bad news.

Eighty percent of people are generally non-confrontational, and telling a person something negative can be confrontational. Giving someone negative feedback doesn't have to be contentious, but 80 percent know it could be. Because of this, they are not willing to take the risk. The 20 percent are comfortable with moderate confrontation levels, so they are willing to tell you the truth, even if their feedback has a negative component to it.

Let's explore why humans are so risk-averse when it comes to sharing negative feedback.

1. People generally try to stay positive. We are taught that positive is good; focus here. Negative is bad; stay away. People generally would like to be seen and viewed as positive rather than negative.
2. People don't feel qualified to give you negative feedback. They don't feel like they have the expertise to tell you they didn't like some aspect of their interaction with you.
3. People may be afraid they will offend you. They are trying to spare you hurt feelings. The nicer you are, the less negative feedback you will get.

225

Leadership: Building and Nurturing a World-Class Team of Massage Therapists

4. Some people don't receiving negative feedback it. So they don't give it.

5. We don't believe in our hearts that someone really wants to hear about what we didn't like. They were just asking to be polite. They were asking a rhetorical question. We think what everyone really wants to hear is all the good stuff. And none of the bad.

6. People are taught from childhood to be positive, to say nice things. "If you don't have something nice to say, don't say anything at all."

7. We don't believe deep down that telling people some negative aspects of our interactions with them will make a difference, other than upset them. We have very little confidence that people can take a negative comment and learn from it to improve themselves.

The above are just some of the reasons it's difficult to get humans to share a negative interaction or some feedback of a negative nature. Positive feedback is another story. Everyone loves to give you positive feedback. Many people will shower you with praise, especially your staff, even if it's not actually true.

You are seeking feedback in a challenging environment. People are much less likely to provide you with negative feedback when you, their boss, hold the keys to their future and livelihood. Now you have changed the game. You no longer have just 20 percent of the people willing to share negative feedback. It drops to somewhere in the 1 percent range.

As a manager, it will be challenging to get your team members to tell you about areas you need to improve in.

So, what's a boss to do?

Create an Environment for Feedback

You have to create an environment for accurate feedback among your staff. How is this done? It requires you to have the following in your workplace culture:

226

Section 7: Honest Conversations

- Openness
- Honesty
- Authenticity
- Vulnerability

- Growth mindset
- Desire to constantly improve

Hopefully have been cultivating these components in your workplace. A workplace where the above qualities are present will form the foundation for your staff to feel comfortable and safe in bringing important items, both negative and positive, to your attention.

Actions you can take to create an open environment for feedback:

1. Do more listening than talking. Feedback is the responsibility of the receiver and not the giver.
2. Pay attention to the physical setup for the conversation. This may mean getting out from behind your big desk.
3. You have to convince your team, through your actions, that there is zero downside in speaking the truth. In other words, no punishment.
4. Give honest feedback to your team. Of course, not all of your feedback will be negative. You will include areas of strengths and areas of relative weakness. You will model the behavior you want them to emulate. Your willingness to step out of your comfort zone and be honest with them will set the stage for them to be open and honest with you.
5. Do not get defensive or try to justify the behavior they are describing. It's imperative to simply listen. Take notes if you desire. Ask for clarification. Ask, "Is there anything else?" When they finish this, give them a heartfelt thank you.
6. Create an anonymous survey. Ask questions about your performance and management style. If you choose this approach, be prepared for brutal honesty, even meanness.

Leadership: Building and Nurturing a World-Class Team of Massage Therapists

7. Create an advisory committee to help you brainstorm areas where you might improve. This often is a good approach if there is a particular area that you want feedback in. People feel safer giving feedback in a group setting.

The Two Questions Steve Jobs Used to Get Brutally Honest Feedback

He would arrange sessions with all the different teams—the *Cars* team and the technology team—so there were a dozen or so people in each session. Then he would point to one person in each session and say, "Tell me what's not working at Pixar." That person might offer something like, "The design team isn't open to the new technology we're building." Jobs would ask others if they agreed. He would then choose someone else and say, "Tell me what's working at Pixar."

If you have the book's digital version, please click the link below for an excellent three-minute snippet on how challenging it can be to get feedback. This is from a Tim Ferris interview with Kevin Systrom, Co-Founder of Instagram on the Difficulty of Getting Feedback.

https://soundcloud.com/user-166537898/feedback-kevin-systrom-tim-ferriss

Considerations When Giving Feedback to the Team

Some professionals say you need to have a praise-to-criticism ratio of 10 to 1. Others advocate the "feedback sandwich"—opening and closing with praise, sticking some criticism in between. I think venture capitalist Ben Horowitz got it right when he called this approach the "shit sandwich." Horowitz suggests that such a technique might work with less-experienced people. Still, I've found the average child sees through it just as clearly as an executive does.

Section 7: Honest Conversations

"Wow, the font you chose for that presentation really blew me away. But the content bordered on the obvious. Still, it really impresses me how neat your desk always is." Patronizing or insincere praise like that will erode trust and hurt your relationships just as much as overly harsh criticism.

Stating Your Intention to be Helpful Can Lower Defenses

When you tell somebody that you really want to help, it can go a long way toward making them receptive to what you're saying. Try a little preamble. For example, in your own words, say something like, "I'm going to describe a problem I see; I may be wrong, and if I am, I hope you'll tell me; if I'm not, I hope my bringing it up will help you fix it."

Give Feedback Immediately

Giving guidance as quickly and as informally as possible is an essential part of radical candor, but it takes discipline—both because of our natural inclination to delay/avoid confrontation and because our days are busy enough as it is. But this is one of those cases where the difference in terms of time spent and impact is enormous. Delay at your peril! If you wait to tell somebody for a week or a quarter, the incident is so far in the past that they can't fix the problem or build on the success.

Say it in 2–3 Minutes Between Meetings

"How do I find the time?" When I (Kim) heard people ask this question, at first, I took this as a sign that they hadn't bought my argument about how important guidance was. But after more conversations, I realized that people actually don't believe it can be quick. They think it's an hour-long conversation they need to schedule. They believe giving useful guidance is going to add hours of meetings to each week. They think of it like a root canal.

Don't Let Stuff Build Up

Unspoken criticism explodes like a dirty bomb. Just as in your personal life, remaining silent at work for too long about something that angers or frustrates you makes it more likely that you will eventually blow up in a way that makes you look irrational

Adapt to an Individual's Preferences

While most people do like to be praised in public, for some, public mention is cruel and unusual punishment. When you're praising people, your goal is to let them know what they did well as clearly as possible and in a way that will make them feel best—not the way you'd like to hear it.

SECTION 8

How to Use This Material on Honest Conversation

Ways This Honest Communication Material Can Make a Difference

When learning about the complexities of honest communication, it's tempting to think it requires lots of memorizing, cue cards, and months to years of formal practice before the ideas here can be useful. I'm happy to report that is not the case. This material can be extremely helpful in your daily communication with no formal training.

Towards the end of the book *Crucial Conversations*, the authors make this encouraging comment: "Our research has shown that you need not be perfect with this material to make major progress."

This has been my experience as well. I've found that merely having a common set of definitions and words to use is often enough to cause real progress to be made.

Having a Shared Set of Definitions and Words

Let's talk for a minute about having a common set of terms, definitions, words, ideas, and principles. This is something I saw happening from

Leadership: Building and Nurturing a World-Class Team of Massage Therapists

the very moment we started to use the term "honest conversation." Team members immediately started to use the term with me, then with other team members. They would approach me and say, "Can we have an honest conversation?" or, "Can I speak to you honestly?" This was before any real discussion or training had occurred in our leadership classes. We, as a team, started having real breakthroughs just because one term was introduced. This was an insight that came unexpectantly and entirely by accident.

I saw the same thing happen when I introduced the concept of creating stories and attaching meaning. All of a sudden, people were using these terms in "normal," everyday discussions. They were communicating ideas and concepts that would have been difficult, perhaps even impossible, before introducing the term.

For example, being able to say, "The story I'm telling myself right now is…" Can have a powerful impact on communicating a challenging idea or communication your position. Using any of the terms and concepts in this book in a shared way will have a surprising effect on our ability as a team to honestly communicate.

Imagine the ability to communicate complex ideas by having a common/shared understanding of concepts such as:

- Armor
- Vulnerability
- Authentic
- Extreme Ownership
- Leadership
- Honest Conversations
- Leading up the chain
- Courage
- Curiosity
- Empathy
- Invisible Army
- Psychological Safety
- Safety
- Shared pool of knowledge
- Fools Choice
- Mutual Purpose
- Mutual Respect
- Master our stories
- The story I am telling myself
- Attaching meaning

- Path to action
- Assuming we know others motivations

- Telling a story
- Creating a story
- Clever stories

In addition to definitions and words, I have attempted to curate and collect as many general principles as possible in the area of authenticity and honest communication. For example, Extreme ownership is a term and a principle. It's an entire philosophy of leadership with far-reaching implications. The same could be said for mastering our stories or attaching meaning. Let's take a moment and summarize what we have learned so far in the area of honest communication.

A Review of Honest Conversations Principles and Concepts

Your Mental State

The first area to get right with honest communication is our own mental state. It's important to understand and be clear on what you hope to gain from the conversation. Make sure your intentions are clear. Before you start, ask yourself, *What is the desired result or outcome I have for this conversation?* Sometimes, the simple act of letting the other person know what you are trying to do goes a long way towards meeting your objective. For example: "I really want to help you present this project in the most positive light. I think it would be better if you…"

Allow Emotions to Settle

Allow time for the emotional charge to dissipate. Frustrations and anger will only create problems and block honest communication. Wait for the emotional charge to go away before trying to address issues. Remember and be mindful of the gap—allow time to let emotions settle. You may

Leadership: Building and Nurturing a World-Class Team of Massage Therapists

need to wait a day or a week or a month until you feel you can have a discussion that is not overly emotionally charged.

Be Careful of Tone

It's often not so much what we say, but how we say it. We communicate with more than words. The tone of our conversation makes a difference. Take care that the tone of your voice is sending the correct message. Ask yourself if your tone is in line with the message you wish to project.

Minimize the Tendency to Confront

Rather than confront immediately, start with the facts, the objective part of the path. Tell about the story you are telling yourself and ask them to help you understand where your story is missing information. Assume you have created an inaccurate story. Ask for clarification and maintain curiosity.

Focus Less on Skills and More on Principles

It's helpful to think of this material as principle-based rather than technique-based. Focus on the general principles more than on how to specifically say something.

Below are ten principles to help you be more effective in your honest communication.

1. **Seek to understand before seeking to be understood.** Remember, it's not enough to understand. The person needs to know you understand. They need to feel understood. This may require them giving a hefty amount of background and verbiage that you may not need. But they need to get it out, so they know you know. This is a super powerful concept. Understanding this will pay dividends way beyond work-related issues.

Section 8: How to Use This Material on Honest Conversation

2. **Watch for safety issues.** If a person feels unsafe, build safety before you move on. Signs that safety is an issue are silence and violence (verbal attacks).

3. **Focus on mutual goals or purpose.**

4. **Focus on mutual respect.** Find something in the other person you can respect.

5. **Accept responsibility.** Act with extreme ownership. Apologize if necessary. Be curious. Don't blame others.

6. **Show appropriate empathy** for others' positions.

7. **Watch for slipping out of useful dialogue** and work to restore it. Learn to look for being in or out of dialogue. If you realize you are no longer contributing to the pool of useful information, you can say, "I think we've moved away from what is important to both of us."

8. **Set yourself up for success.** You would not want to tackle a complex, serious issue with a client at the front desk. Depending on the nature of the issue, set aside time and find an appropriate location where you can have time and privacy to thoroughly discuss the issue. Decide how serious the situation is. Pick the right setting for the situation.

There are different levels of issues you may be dealing with:

- Mild charge: "Would you mind not calling me Susie? My name is Susan."
- Medium level of charge:
- High level of charge:

For medium and high levels of charge, it's probably best to get out of the office. You might choose to meet at the end of a shift or on a day off for both parties.

235

1. **State your path** if it would be helpful and the situation calls for it. Remember, the path looks like this:

Event (facts) → interpretation (or story) → feeling
or emotion → action

2. **Master your stories.** State the facts first, the story second. Share the narrative you have created. Let them know the conclusion you have come to based on the facts.

Given the fact that **humans create stories**, ask yourself,

- Am I aware of the facts of the situation?
- What story have I create based on the facts?
- Have I couched my position of a story that needs clarification?
- Have I understood the other person's story?

Ask yourself, am I telling clever stories?

- **Victim stories:** the other person is bad, wrong, or dumb. We are good, right, or brilliant. In victim stories, we exaggerate our own innocence.
- **Villain stories:** turning normal decent human beings into villains.
- **Helpless Stories:** we are powerless or at the mercy of someone or something.

Rules of Engagement

Below are a couple of rules of engagement for guiding your crucial conversation. You might mention these in passing as the conversation starts, or you could bring them up as you see the need.

Section 8: How to Use This Material on Honest Conversation

Concept of Permission

How do we start the process of honest communication? Give each other and ourselves permission to:

- Speak freely.
- Be honest.
- Listen with curiosity to understand the other person's views and positions.

Challenge other beliefs, perspectives, and assumptions.

- Can we have permission to point out when it looks like assumptions are being made? Assumptions are not always wrong or incorrect, but it may occasionally be useful to point out that it's an assumption, nevertheless.
- Can we have permission to point out when it looks like stories are being created?
- Can we have permission to point out when it looks like someone is attaching meanings to events, words, etc.?

Speaking Freely

Remember, when someone speaks freely, they are being vulnerable, they're taking a risk. We must recognize that when someone speaks, they speak from their own point of view. They are sharing their point of view with you. We must take care not to shut them down or minimize their feelings.

When another person dares to speak freely, we can acknowledge the person for the courage to speak their truth. We can stay curious about what they are feeling and saying. We can voice our own perspective on the issue. Remember to take care not to imply other perspectives are wrong, and ours are right. Ours are just ours. And they are different. We each see through a different lens. We can invite them to see from another point of view. An

237

Leadership: Building and Nurturing a World-Class Team of Massage Therapists

invitation to see something differently feels a lot different than being told you are wrong.

Use Honest Communication Tools

Here is a list of terms and concepts that can be used as you approach honest conversations:

- **Circle back.** Circling back allows us to revisit a conversation or interaction after we've had time to fully process it. "I need to think about this. Can we circle back tomorrow?"
- **Say more.** Seek to understand first. You may need a deeper understanding of the issue at hand. "Please tell me more about that."
- **Timeout.** "Let's take a break and circle back."
- **Support.** "What does support from me look like to you? How would you describe it?"
- **Curiosity.** "I'm curious about…"
- **Story.** "That's not my experience…" or, "This is how I am seeing it."
- **Help me understand.** "Help me understand your thinking behind this."

Good questions to discuss as a team regarding honest communication philosophy:

- When could these honest communication concepts be used?
- When should they not be used?
- When will using these ideas have the greatest potential for problems?
- Honest conversation does not mean "spilling" (dumping) on a co-worker.
- Effective honest conversations lack aggressiveness.

Section 8: How to Use This Material on Honest Conversation

- How do we keep team members who are comfortable with conflict from being too aggressive or bullying more passive team members?
- It should be culturally acceptable to **not accept** an invitation for an honest conversation. In other words, we are not going to force someone to have an honest conversation. It should be mutually agreeable to both parties.

One parameter we may choose to place on this material is that it be used for **interpersonal issues** rather than **performance issues**. Remember we said those were two broad categories of workplace conflict, interpersonal and workplace. With this as a guideline, we would leave correcting workplace performance and workplace discipline to the managers who have:

- **Rapport** with team members.
- **Special training** to deal with sensitive issues.
- **Authority** to give corrective feedback and ask for behavioral changes.

The material presented in this book is meant to be a starting point for allowing honest communication to occur more often in our workplace. Much practical learning will need to take place in the real world of real people. With this material as a beginning point, we can start the journey to have more honest, authentic conversations. There will be a lot of midcourse corrections along this path.

These principles will guide you both in your personal life and your professional life. Please feel free to read the books I've outlined here to expand your knowledge of this material.

I wish you much success in your quest to have open and honest conversations.

Appendix 1

Leadership Principles from Wooden on Leadership by Coach John Wooden

On Success

"Success is peace of mind in knowing you have made the effort to become the best of which you are capable. Effort is the ultimate measure of your success."

On Our Potential

"Most of us have potential far beyond what we think possible."

On the Competition

"Don't lose sleep worrying about the competition. Let the competition lose sleep worrying about you."

On the Example of The Leader

"I believe there is no more powerful leadership tool than your own personal example. In almost every way, the team ultimately becomes a reflection of their leader."

Leadership: Building and Nurturing a World-Class Team of Massage Therapists

On Love for Your Team

"I believe you must have love in your heart for the people under your leadership. I did."

A Player on Coach Wooden

"Coach Wooden never thought he knew everything. He never thought his way was the only way. He was always searching for ways to improve."

On Showing Appreciation

"Many managers and coaches take for granted that the people who work for them know how their efforts impact the organization. This is especially true for those in lesser roles. Go out of your way to make them feel included. Thank them for their efforts. Explain why their work matters and how it helps the business to be successful."

On Fundamentals

"Fundamentals, well done, are the foundation upon which effective leaders build highly productive teams. There was no one thing that made the UCLA basketball team champions, it was hundreds of small things done the right way and done consistently."

On Time Management

"Make every day your masterpiece."

On the Purpose of a Leader

"You might say a leader has a simple mission, to get those under his guidance to consistently perform at their peak level."

Section 8: How to Use This Material on Honest Conversation

On the Infection of Success

"Success breeds satisfaction, and satisfaction breeds failure. You will continue to achieve only if you do not permit the infection of success to take hold of your organization. The symptom of that infection is called complacency. Contentment with past accomplishments or acceptance of the status quo can derail an organization."

A Player on Coach Wooden Winning

"Coach Wooden didn't talk about winning, ever. He taught us to always give the best you've got. That's the goal. Winning was never mentioned."

On Feedback

"A leader must know how to deliver feedback and criticism, and he must also teach those under his leadership how to receive criticism."

Appendix 2

Mindset: The New Psychology to Success by Carol Dweck, Psychologist, Stanford University

Over the next few pages, I have summarized this amazing book. We lovingly call this book The Oak Haven Bible. I believe it holds the key to a frame of mind that allows people to learn, grow, and develop. I further believe that the growth mindset spoken of in this book is the most important factor in a fully functioning team. I encourage you to read the book.

Carol studied children as they were asked to try to put together increasingly difficult puzzles. She noticed two different general responses.

- One group became discouraged as the puzzles became harder and harder.
- The other group seemed to roll up their sleeves and say, "Bring it on." They seemed to thrive on a challenge, even if they were no more successful than the first group.

This initial observation led to a series of experiments spanning many years and, eventually, she reported her work in a landmark book *Mindset*.

In the book, Dweck speaks of the ongoing controversy related to human talent and intelligence. Were these characteristics fixed, set from birth? Or were they qualities that could be developed and nurtured?

Think about an Einstein or a Michael Jordan.

Leadership: Building and Nurturing a World-Class Team of Massage Therapists

Is IQ Fixed in Our DNA, or Can it Be Developed Through Effort on Our Part?

French psychologist Alfred Binet, inventor of the IQ Test, said, "A few modern philosophers…assert that an individual's intelligence is a fixed quantity, a quantity which cannot be increased. We must protest and react against this brutal pessimism. With practice, training, and, above all, method, we manage to increase our attention, our memory, our judgment, and literally become more intelligent than we were before."

Robert Sternberg, the present-day guru of intelligence, writes that the major factor in whether people achieve expertise "is not some fixed prior ability, but purposeful engagement." Or, as his forerunner Binet recognized, it's not always the people who start out the smartest who end up the smartest.

So, which is it?

- Fixed—as in our DNA is fixed from birth
- Growth—we can develop skills, intelligence, and talents through individual work or struggle.

Dweck's work showed that the answer is that both are correct.

What Determines Where You Are on the Spectrum → Belief (Mindset)

Dweck's research identified two distinct mindsets that determine how our talents, skills, abilities will unfold over our lifetime.

The Fixed Mindset – believing your qualities are carved in stone.

- You have a fixed amount of intelligence from birth
- You have a certain personality from birth
- You have a fixed moral character from birth

246

Section 8: How to Use This Material on Honest Conversation

CHARACTERISTICS OF A FIXED MINDSET

- Concerned with how you will be judged
- Not starting a task if you think there is a high chance of failure
- "Failure" means I'm inadequate at some level
- Always trying to prove themselves
- Sensitive about being "wrong."
- Failure means – I have not fulfilled my potential
- Failure means – I am not "smart" or talented; if you were smart or talented, you would not have to work hard.
- When they succeed – they often feel a sense of superiority – since it means that their fixed traits are better than someone else.

The Growth Mindset – believing the qualities you have at birth are just the starting point for growth and development.

- Any human characteristic can be cultivated and developed through life.
- Everyone can change and grow through application and experience.

CHARACTERISTICS OF A GROWTH MINDSET

- Passion for stretching beyond what you are currently capable of.
- Sticking with it – even when it's not going well
- Being willing to "fail" knowing that what you learn in the process will be extremely valuable going forward.
- Concerned with Improving
- Effort is what makes you smart or talented, and "I control the effort expended."
- People in a growth mindset don't just seek challenge – they thrive on it.

247

Leadership: Building and Nurturing a World-Class Team of Massage Therapists

- No matter your ability, it's effort that ignites that ability and turns it into accomplishment.
- Abilities can be cultivated through effort.

Psychologist Benjamin Barber said, "I don't divide the world into the weak and the strong—or the successes and the failures. I divide the world into the learners and non-learners."

Dweck's research showed that people with different mindsets looked for someone totally different in a mate.

A fixed mindset ideal mate would:

- Put them on a pedestal.
- Make them feel perfect.
- Worship them.

In other words, someone would reinforce their fixed qualities.

A growth mindset ideal mate would:

- See their faults and help them work on them.
- Challenge them to become a better person.
- Encourage them to learn new things.

I would argue that we all have fixed mindset capacities. Still, the mindset we adopt allows us to maximize the abilities and capacities we have.

Are Mindsets a Permanent Part of Our Makeup, Or Can We Change Them?

"Mindsets are an important part of your personality, but you can change them. Just by knowing about the two mindsets, you can start thinking and reacting in new ways. People tell me they start to catch themselves when they are in the throes of the fixed mindset—passing up a chance for learning, feeling labeled as a failure, or getting discouraged when something requires a lot of effort. And then they switch themselves into the growth mindset—making sure they take the challenge, learn from the failure, or continue their effort. When my graduate students and I first discovered the mindsets, they would catch me in the fixed mindset and scold me. It's also important to realize that even if people have a fixed mindset, they're not always in that mindset. In fact, in many of our studies, we *put* people into a growth mindset. We tell them that an ability can be learned and that the task will give them a chance to do that. Or we have them read a scientific article that teaches them the growth mindset. The article describes three people who did not have natural ability but who developed exceptional skills. These experiences make our research participants into growth-minded thinkers, at least for the moment, and they act like growth-minded thinkers, too."

Can I Be Half and Half? I Recognize Both Mindsets in Myself.

"Many people have elements of both. People can also have different mind-sets in different areas. I might think that my artistic skills are fixed but that my intelligence can be developed. Or that my personality is fixed, but my creativity can be developed. We've found that whatever mindset people have in a particular area will guide them in that area."

As I read *Mindsets* and became more and more fascinated with the different mindsets and how they color our world and our experiences, I wondered how mindsets come to be and how they could change.

At least some of the challenge I had as a coach at Oak Haven was being impacted by therapists who were locked in the fixed mindset:

- Afraid to try new things
- Resistant to recommendations for change
- Defensive
- Offended if I implied they needed to work on an area

Where does mindset come from?

- Instilled in us by our parents, early teachers, and other people in our early life that had an influence on us.
- Instilled over time, mostly without our knowledge.
- Praising children's ability rather than the effort expended sends them into a fixed mindset.

"Every word and action from parent to child sends a message. Listen to what you say to your kids and tune in to the messages you're sending. Are they messages that say, "You have permanent traits, and I'm judging them"? Or are they messages that say, "You're a developing person and I'm interested in your development"? How do you use praise? Remember that praising children's intelligence or talent or looks, as tempting as it is, sends a fixed-mindset message. It makes their confidence and motivation more fragile. Instead, try to focus on the processes they used – their strategies, effort, or choices. Practice working the process of praise into your interactions with your children."

Can a Mindset Be Changed?

Yes. The way we praise someone sends a message.

- "You learned that so quickly, you are so smart." Now the child thinks, *If I don't learn quickly, I'm not smart.*
- "Wow, you are brilliant. You got an A on that test without even studying." Now the child thinks, *If I have to study, I'm not that smart.*

It's the kids with a fixed mindset, the vulnerable kids, who are obsessed with this. Wouldn't harping on intelligence or talent make kids even more obsessed with it?

After seven experiments with hundreds of children, we had some of the clearest findings I've ever seen: praising children's intelligence harms their motivation and it harms their performance. How can that be? Don't

Section 8: How to Use This Material on Honest Conversation

children love to be praised? Yes, children love praise. And they especially love to be praised for their intelligence and talent. It really does give them a boost, a special glow—but only for a moment. The minute they hit a snag, their confidence goes out the window, and their motivation hits rock bottom. If success means they're smart, then failure means they're dumb. That's the fixed mindset.

Does this mean we can't praise our children enthusiastically when they do something great? Should we try to restrain our admiration for their successes? Not at all. It just means that we should keep away from a certain kind of praise...praise that judges their intelligence or talent. Or praise that implies that we're proud of them for their intelligence or talent rather than for the work they put in. We can praise them as much as we want for the growth-oriented process—what they accomplished through practice, study, persistence, and good strategies. And we can ask them about their work in a way that admires and appreciates their efforts and choices.

"You really studied for your test, and your improvement shows it. You read the material over several times, you outlined it, and you tested yourself on it. It really worked!" "I like the way you tried all kinds of strategies on that math problem until you finally got it. You thought of a lot of different ways to do it and found the one that worked!" "I like that you took on that challenging project for your science class. It will take a lot of work—researching, designing the apparatus, buying the parts, and building it. Boy, you're going to learn a lot of great things." "I know school used to be easy for you, and you used to feel like the smart kids all the time. But the truth is that you weren't using your brain to the fullest. I am really excited about how you're stretching yourself now and working to learn hard things." "That homework was so long and involved. I really admire the way you concentrated and finished it" "That picture has so many beautiful colors. Tell me about them." "You put so much thought into this essay. It really makes me understand Shakespeare in a new way." "The passion you put into that piano piece gives me a real feeling of joy. How do you feel when you play it?"

251

Leadership: Building and Nurturing a World-Class Team of Massage Therapists

What about a student who worked hard and didn't do well? "I liked the effort you put in, but let's work together some more and figure out what it is you don't understand." "We all have different learning curves. It may take more time for you to catch on to this and be comfortable with this material, but if you keep at it like this, you will." "Everyone learns a different way. Let's keep trying to find the way that works for you."

Messages About Failure

"Praising success should be the least of our problems, right? Failure seems like a much more delicate matter. Children may already feel discouraged and vulnerable. Let's tune in again, this time to the message parents can send in times of failure. Nine-year-old Elizabeth was on her way to her first gymnastics meet. Lanky, flexible, and energetic, she was just right for gymnastics, and she loved it. Of course, she was a little nervous about competing, but she was good at gymnastics and felt confident of doing well. She had even thought about the perfect place in her room to hang the ribbon she would win. In the first event, the floor exercises, Elizabeth went first. Although she did a nice job, the scoring changed after the first few girls, and she lost. Elizabeth also did well in the other events, but not well enough to win. By the end of the evening, she had received no ribbons and was devastated. What would you do if you were Elizabeth's parents?"

- Tell Elizabeth you thought she was the best.
- Tell her she was robbed of a ribbon that was rightfully hers.
- Reassure her that gymnastics is not that important.
- Tell her she has the ability and will surely win next time.
- Tell her she didn't deserve to win.

There is a strong message in our society about how to boost children's self-esteem, and the central part of that message is: Protect them from failure! While this may help with the immediate problem of a child's disappointment, it can be harmful in the long run. Why?

252

Section 8: How to Use This Material on Honest Conversation

Let's look at the five possible reactions from a mindset point of view:

- The first is basically insincere. She was not the best—you know it, and she does too. This offers her no recipe for how to recover or how to improve.
- The second places blame on others, when, in fact, the problem was mostly with her performance, not the judges. Do you want her to grow up blaming others for her deficiencies?
- The third teaches her to devalue something if she doesn't do well in it right away. Is this really the message you want to send?
- The fourth may be the most dangerous message of all. Does ability automatically take you where you want to go? If Elizabeth didn't win this meet, why should she win the next one?
- The last option seems hardhearted under the circumstances. And, of course, you wouldn't say it quite that way. But that's pretty much what her growth-minded father told her. Here's what he actually said, "Elizabeth, I know how you feel. It's so disappointing to have your hopes up and to perform your best but not to win. But you know, you haven't really earned it yet. There were many girls there who've been in gymnastics longer than you and who've worked a lot harder than you. If this is something you really want, then it's something you'll really have to work for."

He also let Elizabeth know that if she wanted to do gymnastics purely for fun, that was just fine. But if she wanted to excel in the competitions, more was required. Elizabeth took this to heart, spending much more time repeating and perfecting her routines, especially her weakest events. At the next meet, there were 80 girls from all over the region. Elizabeth won five ribbons for individual events. She was the overall champion of the competition, hauling home a giant trophy. By now, her room is so covered with awards, you can hardly see the walls.

253

Leadership: Building and Nurturing a World-Class Team of Massage Therapists

Her father told her the truth and taught her how to learn from her failures. He taught her what it takes to succeed in something you care about. He sympathized deeply with her disappointment, but he did not give her a phony boost that would only lead to further disappointment.

I've met with many coaches who ask me: "What happened to the coachable athletes? Where did they go?" Many of the coach's lament that, when they give their athletes corrective feedback, they grumble that their confidence is being undermined. Sometimes the athletes phone home and complain to their parents. They seem to want coaches who will simply tell them how talented they are and leave it at that.

In the old days, the coaches say that after a little league game or a kiddie soccer game, parents used to review and analyze the game on the way home and give helpful (process) tips. Now on the ride home, they say, parents heap blame on the coaches and referees for the child's poor performance or the team's loss. They don't want to harm the child's confidence by putting the blame on the child.

But as in the example of Elizabeth above, children need honest and constructive feedback. If children are protected from it, they won't learn well. They will experience advice, coaching, and feedback as negative and undermining. Withholding constructive criticism does not help children's confidence; it harms their future.

How Do You Change a Mindset?

How do you use praise? Remember that praising children's intelligence or talent or looks, tempting as it is, sends a fixed-mindset message. It makes their confidence and motivation more fragile. Instead, try to focus on the processes they used—their strategies, efforts, or choices. Practice working the process praise into your interactions with your children.

Appendix 3

Multipliers by Liz Wiseman

The Gallup organization Global Workplace Study found across 142 countries, only 13 percent of people worldwide are fully engaged at work.

Do what you have to do to make sure you're not one of these people who lack full engagement. We spend too much time at work to be unengaged, disinterested, and uncaring.

Wiseman noticed there were specific practices that caused increased engagement and other practices that caused decreased engagement.

People across cultures, professions, and industries come to work each day hoping to be well utilized, not by being given more and more work, but by recognizing that they are capable of contributing in significant ways and doing more challenging work.

There is more intelligence inside our organizations than we are using. This realization led to the idea that there was a type of leader who Wiseman called Multipliers. These were leaders who saw, used, and grew the intelligence of others. She also noticed another kind of leader, whom she labeled Diminishers. These diminishing leaders shut down the intelligence of those around them.

The vast majority of the diminishing happening inside our workplace is done with the best of intentions, by what Wiseman calls the "accidental diminisher." These are good people trying to be good managers but falling short.

Leadership: Building and Nurturing a World-Class Team of Massage Therapists

Some leaders make us better and smarter. They bring out our intelligence. They are leaders who access and revitalize the intelligence in the people around them. They are called multipliers.

Some leaders seem to drain the intelligence and capability out of the people around them. For them to look smart, other people have to look dumb. When they walk into the room, the shared IQ drops, and the length of the meeting doubles. In countless settings, these leaders are the idea killers and energy destroyers. Around these leaders, intelligence flows only one way, from them to others. These people are called diminishers.

The multipliers use their intelligence as a tool rather than a weapon. They apply their intelligence to amplify the smarts and the capabilities of people around them. People get smarter and better in their presence. Ideas grow, challenges are overcome, and hard problems are solved. When these leaders walk into the room, light bulbs start switching on over people's heads. Ideas would flow so fast you'd have to replay the meeting in slow motion just to see what was going on. These leaders act like amplifiers. They are intelligence amplifiers.

You could say there are two types of managers. Manager number one is the genius maker. They grow people's intelligence. They are not the center of attention and don't worry about how smart they look; what they worry about is extracting the smarts and effort from each member of their team. Manager number two is the genius. These managers hire intelligent people, but their people soon realize they don't have permission to think for themselves. It isn't how much you know that matters. What matters is how much access you have to what other people know. Multipliers are genius makers. What we mean is that they make everyone around them smarter and more capable. The impact of a multiplier can be seen in two ways. First, with people they work with. And second, with the organizations they shape and create. Multipliers give more than their jobs require and volunteer their discretionary effort.

Multipliers get more from people than the people knew they had. The implication of research is that intelligence itself can grow.

Section 8: How to Use This Material on Honest Conversation

Picture children at a buffet line. They load up on food, but a lot of it is left on the plate uneaten. The food gets picked at and pushed around, but much is left to go to waste. Like these children, diminishers are eager to load up on resources (people), and they might even get the job done. Still, many people are left unused, their capability wasted.

The Mind of a Diminisher

The diminisher's view of intelligence is based on elitism and scarcity. Diminishers believe really intelligent people are a rare breed and that they themselves are of that rare breed. Other people will never figure things out without them. In addition to seeing intelligence as a scarce commodity, diminishers regard intelligence as something basic about a person that can't change much. They believe it is static, not able to change over time or circumstance.

The Mind of a Multiplier

Multipliers don't see the world where just a few people deserve to do the thinking. Multipliers see intelligence as continually developing. This observation is consistent with what Carol Dweck calls a growth mindset. They believe that basic qualities, like intelligence and ability, can be cultivated through effort. They assume that people are smart and will figure it out. In what way is this person smart? In answering this question, the multiplier finds capabilities often hidden just below the surface. Multipliers see their job as bringing the right people together in an environment that liberates everyone's best thinking, and then to get out of their way and let them do it.

It's interesting to note how the concepts in *Multiplier* (with the two opposing forces of multiplier and diminisher), are very much in alignment with Dweck's book *Mindset*.

Wiseman's concept of a diminisher, the belief that intelligence is a rare commodity, something you either have or you don't, aligns very well with Dweck's idea of a fixed mindset. And many of the multiplier qualities are

Leadership: Building and Nurturing a World-Class Team of Massage Therapists

very similar to the growth mindset group in Dweck's work. Both authors have amazing insights based on their respective models. Both have a lot to offer the leader and manager of teams.

Five Disciplines of the Multiplier

1. Attract and Optimize Talent

The diminisher is an empire builder who acquires resources and then wastes them. The multiplier is a talent magnet who utilizes and increases everyone's genius.

Multipliers look for talent everywhere. Appreciate all types of genius, along the lines of Daniel Goleman's multiple intelligences. A talent magnet knows that genius comes in many forms.

Multipliers look for native talent or native genius. Native talent is something that people do, not only exceptionally well, but absolutely naturally. **Finding someone's native genius is a key that unlocks discretionary effort.**

Once a multiplier sees the natural talent in a team member, the next step is to label it. Often, people aren't aware of their genius. Simply putting a label on it is enough to open up this genius. By telling people what you see, you can raise their awareness and confidence, allowing them to provide and explore their talent more fully.

The diminisher puts people in boxes and let talent languish. They do no manage their talent.

2. Liberate the Talent

Create an environment that requires your team's best thinking. One thing you can do to liberate talent is become a better listener and talk less.
Other practices of the liberator include creating space for optimal work, demanding the best work from your team, and generating rapid learning cycles, including admitting and sharing mistakes.

Section 8: How to Use This Material on Honest Conversation

3. Extend Challenges

The diminisher is a know-it-all who gives directions. The multiplier is a challenger who defines opportunities and extends challenges to their team to extract the best from the team member.

4. Debate Decisions

Diminishers are decision-makers who try to sell their decisions to others. Multipliers are debate makers who use other brains to explore problems and come to better solutions.

5. Instill Ownership and Accountability

The diminisher is a micromanager who jumps in and out. The multiplier is an investor who gives others ownership and full accountability.

The Accidental Diminisher

Accidental diminishers are managers with the best of intentions. They are good people who think they are doing a good job leading. We all have accidental diminisher moments.

The following are several archetypes of accidental diminishers.

The Idea Guy

This type of leader is a creative, innovative thinker who loves an idea-rich environment. He is a veritable fountain of ideas. Ideas bubble up for him 24/7, so he frequently bursts into the office brimming with new ideas to share with colleagues. This leader doesn't necessarily think his ideas are superior, he simply believes that the more he tosses around his ideas, the more he will spark ideas in others. What actually happens around the idea guy? The ideas he tosses seem compelling to the team, so they begin to chase them. But as soon as they begin to make progress on yesterday's idea, the next day brings a new idea. They realize that they always end up back at

259

Leadership: Building and Nurturing a World-Class Team of Massage Therapists

square one. So why not just stay at square one. As they learn to stop acting on the leader's ideas, they also stop trying to develop their own ideas. After all, if they actually needed a new idea, they could just wait for the fountain to spew. It's easy to get idea lazy around people who are idea-rich. If you've built a reputation as a big thinker, don't be surprised if people save the big thinking for you.

The Energizer

This dynamic, charismatic leader exudes energy. She is always engaged, always present, and always has something to say. These are the leaders with big personalities that can fill a room. They assume that their energy is contagious, like a virus to be caught by anyone in their presence. But, like the common cold, this leader can be draining. She takes away energy rather than providing energy to the people around her. As she expands, like a gas, consuming all the available oxygen, others suffocate. Most team members just find her exhausting. People soon avoid making eye contact or having encounters with her. They think, *I just don't have the energy right now.* And all too often, around this leader, thinking is suppressed.

What do we do around a leader who is always on, the one who lacks an off switch? If you can't find a dimmer switch, you simply turn her off inside your head. You put her in the background, she becomes white noise. Her endless spray of speech becomes muffled and sometimes completely unheard by the people she leads. The energizer thinks she is playing big. But actually, she becomes small, and she makes everyone around her small as well. Her energy isn't contagious; it's numbing. When the leader is always on, everyone else is always off.

The Rescuer

The rescuer is a good manager and a decent person. The rescuer is the type of leader who doesn't like to see people struggle and make avoidable mistakes. At the first sign of distress, he jumps in and helps. Occasionally, he

Section 8: How to Use This Material on Honest Conversation

swoops in with a big heroic rescue. More often, though, he simply lends a hand, resolves the problem, and helps people cross the finish line. This is the most common way leaders accidentally diminish.

The intention of the rescuer is noble. He wants to see other people be successful. He desires to protect the reputation of the people who work for him. Still, because he interrupts a natural performance cycle, he starves people from the vital learning they need to be successful.

When the manager helps too soon and too often, people around him become dependent and helpless. Instead of feeling successful, employees experience frustration and depleted confidence when they fail to cross the finish line. As leaders, sometimes we are most helpful when we don't help.

The Protector

If the leader continually protects people from danger, they never learn to fend for themselves. Natural consequence is a powerful teacher.

Are You an Accidental Diminisher?

Wiseman is careful to clarify that having any of the above-described tendencies does not make you a diminisher. It merely increases the likelihood that you will have a diminishing impact. That's good news. The bad news is that when you have a diminishing impact, you're likely to be completely unaware of it…and probably the last to know.

Here are some questions to ask yourself about whether or not you might be having a diminishing impact.

- How might I be shutting down others' ideas and actions, despite having the best of intentions?
- What am I inadvertently doing that might be having a diminishing impact on others?
- How might my intentions be interpreted differently by others?
- What messages might my actions actually be conveying?

261

Leadership: Building and Nurturing a World-Class Team of Massage Therapists

Becoming a multiplier often starts with becoming less of a diminisher. Becoming a multiplier requires us to understand how our most noble intentions can have a diminishing affect, sometimes deeply so.

When Your Leader is a Diminisher

What happens if you're being led by a diminisher? What can you do?

The first thing to note is that it's impossible to diminish someone out of being a diminisher. You must take on a multiplier role to help someone who leads you out of diminishing tendencies.

Dr. Martin Luther King Junior famously said,

> "The ultimate weakness of violence is that it is a descending spiral, begetting the very thing it seeks to destroy. Instead of diminishing evil, it multiplies it. Returning violence for violence multiplies violence, adding deeper darkness to a night already devoid of stars. Darkness cannot drive out darkness; only light can do that."

When dealing with a diminisher, you can hope and even dream that this person will become a multiplier, and perhaps she will. Or you can choose to be a multiplier yourself.

Research has shown that people can serve as multipliers from any direction, even upward to a diminishing supervisor.

Becoming a Multiplier

Start with your assumptions. **Behavior follows assumptions.** You can knock out a whole set of behaviors by adopting a multiplier mindset.

Another Benefit

Choosing how you lead (multiplier versus diminisher) is not only important for your organization and the people you lead; it can matter to you as

262

Section 8: How to Use This Material on Honest Conversation

well. Multipliers find that, as they bring out the best in others, they also bring out the best in themselves.

Multiplier Mindset

Be small more often. Being small allows others the chance to be big. By being big less often, your ideas will become more powerful and impactful.

Frequently Asked Questions

Question: Are people either diminishers or multipliers, or are there people in the middle?

Answer: The diminisher/multiplier model is a continuum with a few people at the extremes and most everyone else somewhere in between.

Question: Could I be a diminisher to some people and a multiplier to others?

Answer: Yes. The secret to understanding this dynamic is to better understand the assumptions you hold about different people you lead.

Question: Are there times, particularly during a crisis, when diminishing leadership is called for?

Answer: Yes, there are situations when this type of leadership can be helpful. When this does happen, treat these situations like true exceptions. Let the people know that you are taking a different approach at this time.

Acknowledgments

MY HEARTFELT THANKS AND APPRECIATION TO ALLISON MORENO, Lindsey Hoggard, TJ Goddard, and Randy Betker, who helped flush out ideas and edit this manuscript. Their feedback has been extremely helpful in making the final version much more understandable and readable.

Made in the USA
Monee, IL
19 March 2021